Life is a Journey

Dr. Bill Mounce

Brought to you by your friends at

Because spiritual growth matters

Life is a Journey
Copyright © 2016 Bill Mounce and BiblicalTraining.org

Requests for information should be addressed to:
BiblicalTraining, PO 28428,Spokane, WA 99228

ISBN-13: 978-1533664990
ISBN-10: 1533664994
BISAC: Religion / Christianity / General

Printed in the United States of America

16 17 18 19 20 21 22 23 24 25 / 12 11 10 9 8 7 6 5 4 3 2 1

https://www.biblicaltraining.org/life-journey/bill-mounce

Table of Contents

This book is a the transcript of the author's lectures found at

https://www.biblicaltraining.org/life-journey/bill-mounce

Since they are transcripts, they will read like he speaks, not like he writes.

1

Starting your New Life

I would like to begin by talking with you, the new believer, about your conversion. I would like to celebrate your decision, see if you have any basic questions, and fill out your understanding of what happened when you became a disciple of Jesus Christ — a child of God. If you're unsure of anything I say, please ask the person sitting next to you, and they will explain it to you. Also, understand that over the next eleven weeks, I'm going to be spelling out the details about which I'm talking today.

While there are many verses or passages to which I could go, I'd like to base my talk on the most famous verse of all times, the one saying of Jesus that more people know around this world, and that is John 3:1. "For God so loved the world, that he gave his only son, that whoever believes in him will not perish but will have everlasting life." As I talk through your conversion experience, I'd like to use John 3:16 and break it down in pieces.

"FOR GOD SO LOVED THE WORLD"

Notice that Jesus' starting point is the fact that there is a God. God is not some impersonal force, fate, or Mother Nature. God is a personal God who loves; this loving God created the world and created people to inhabit the world. The Bible says he created people in his image, so that among other things, we could have fellowship with our Creator and have a relationship with him. A dog can't live in a relationship with God. You and I were created in his image, and we were made to live in fellowship, in communion, in relationship with our Creator. Our first parents, Adam and Eve, walked in the garden with God. Regardless of what we might hear, creation is no accident, nor are we global freak-chances-of-nature; we are not primal scum that washed up on the shore and then over millions of years became human beings.

We were created as the apex of all creation. We were created intentionally by God. The creation story in Genesis 1 and 2 (the first two chapters in the Bible) is all pointing to the creation of human beings. You and I were created with meaning and purpose; part of that meaning and purpose is that we live in fellowship, in communion, and in relationship with our Creator. Then something terrible happened to this world, and we need to know that God wasn't surprised; God knew this was going to happen before he created anything, yet he still created everything. Adam and Eve, our first parents, were given one lousy, little rule: of all the trees in the garden, you can't eat the fruit of that one tree. I wonder how many times in heaven Adam is going to have to apologize, "I know, I'm sorry, I'm sorry. All I had to do was just one thing…" I'm glad I'm not Adam. There was only one rule he had to follow. By following that one rule, it was a way he and his wife would be demonstrating how much they loved God. By following God's rule, they were saying, "Yes, we live in submission to your Lordship." "You are God and we are not." Yet as we read in Genesis chapter 3, Adam and Eve deliberately chose to break that one rule — they sinned and ate the fruit of that one tree.

The consequence of that sin is they became separated from God. They were separated physically by being kicked out of the garden, but in their hearts they were also separated from God. They were hostile to him and they were alienated from him. The prophet Isaiah says, "But your iniquities have made a separation between you and your God, and your sins have hidden his face from you so that he does not hear" (Isaiah 59:2). We are separated from our holy God, our holy Creator; that is the consequence of sin. The punishment for living separated from God is death; it is in fact, eternal separation.

The Bible says, "the wages of sin is death," eternal separation from God. What was true for Adam and Eve is now true for all people. The Bible says, "all have sinned and fall short of the glory of God." All have committed sin, all have done what God has called us not to do, therefore all of us, apart from the work of Christ that we will learn about in a second, live separate, alienated and hostile lives from our Creator. Our God, while he is a God of love, is also a God of justice. A God of justice cannot allow sin against a holy God to go unpunished, so there is punishment for sin and separation. Yet the good news is that God is also a God of love just as much as he is a God of justice.

"THAT HE GAVE HIS ONLY SON"

Jesus continues in John 3:16, "God so loved the world that he gave." This is how he loved: he gave his only son. He gave his only son to live on earth to live a perfect life and to die on the cross.

What actually happened on the cross

What actually happened on the cross? What happened was more than a man just dying. Jesus lived a life of perfection. Jesus lived a life without sin. So when he died, his death was not payment for his own sin, because he had not committed sin, but his death became payment for your sin and my sin. Because his death became the penalty for our sin, forgiveness is now available.

The prophet Isaiah, 700 or so years ago before the time of Christ, wrote down what was going to happen on the cross; it is an amazing prophecy. "Surely he," meaning Jesus, "has borne our griefs and carried our sorrows; yet we esteemed him stricken, smitten by God, and afflicted." Jesus carries our griefs and our sorrows and we think God is mad at him. "But he," Jesus, "was wounded for our transgressions; he was crushed for our iniquities; upon him was the chastisement," the punishment, "that brought us peace, and with his stripes, we are healed. All we like sheep have gone astray; we have turned everyone to his own way; and the Lord has laid on him," on Jesus, "the iniquity," the sin, "of us all" (Isaiah 53:4-6). Later on in the New Testament, the apostle Paul writes that "while we were yet sinners, Christ died for us."

Jesus lived a perfect life. His death was not penalty for his own sin, and therefore, his death became the means of God's forgiving your sin and my sin. Forgiveness is available. Because of our sin, there is a chasm that exists between God and us. Jesus' death on the cross bridged that chasm. Jesus, on the cross, made a relationship with God possible. Jesus, on the cross, made it possible for you and me to go home to the garden and walk once again with God.

When I hear that, one of the questions in my mind is: How on earth is that possible? (Although, when you think about it, the answer is not on earth.) How is it possible for one man's death to pay the penalty for the sin of all men, women, and children? How is that possible? The answer is, "I don't know." The Bible never fully explains how that's possible, but it at least gives us two parts of the answer of how it is possible for Jesus' death to pay the penalty for our sin.

1. Merciful heart of God

One of the answers is simply that it's buried deep in the merciful heart of God; it's because of God's mercy and grace. You and I don't deserve to be forgiven. Jesus asks, "What can a man give in exchange for his soul?" The answer is nothing; you and I have nothing we can do. No amount of religious activity and no amount of being better than our neighbors is enough to gain forgiveness of our sin; the answer is deeply buried down inside the merciful heart of God.

We understand that we don't deserve salvation; but God, in his goodness and his mercy toward undeserving sinners, decided that the death of an innocent sacrifice could pay the penalty of another person's sin — that's mercy! Throughout the Old Testament up to the cross, the entire sacrificial system is designed to teach us that the death of an innocent sacrifice can pay the penalty of another's sin because God is a merciful God.

2. Who Jesus is

The other part to the answer of how it is possible that Jesus' death pays the penalty for your sin and my sin is wrapped up in who Jesus is. Jesus is fully God; Jesus is fully human, and it is because of the incarnation that he was able to bear the sin of the world and pay the penalty for your sin and my sin.

If I lived a sinless life, and then died, I couldn't pay the price for your sin, could I? Jesus had to be fully God, because only God could bear the weight of the penalty of all sin. When Jesus hung on the cross, God made him sin, the Bible says. It's not just that he was punished, but he actually was made to be sin. Jesus was made to be all sin that all people of all time ever committed or ever will commit. No human being could ever bare that weight; at every level, it would be impossible. Jesus had to be God in order to bear the weight of all of your sin, all my sin, and the sin of all the people throughout all the ages.

Yet there is also something in God's heart that says that if you are going to provide a sacrifice for human beings, you also have to be a human being. Therefore, Jesus had to become fully human if he were to bear sin of all human beings. In the book of Hebrews, the author writes, "Therefore Jesus had to be made like his brothers in every respect, so that he could provide propitiation, so that he could provide a sacrifice for your sin." I don't fully understand how Jesus' death could pay the penalty for my sin much less yours. However, I do know that it's wrapped up in the merciful heart of God, and that God had to provide the sacrifice himself, but he had to provide it as a human being in order to forgive the sin of all human beings.

"THAT WHOEVER BELIEVES IN HIM"

"God so loved the world, that he gave his only son..." And then Jesus, in John 3:16, moves to our response, "that whoever believes in him"

Whoever believes

That word, "whoever," is really important. It tells us that no one is beyond Jesus' ability to save. When Jesus cried out from the cross his last words, "it is finished," and then bowed his head in death, he meant what he said. He had completed the task for which God the Father had sent him to earth; that is, to be the sacrifice for the sin of people. He did his job well; he completed it; he finished it. Now, when we cry out for forgiveness, no matter what we have done and no matter what we will do, God is able to forgive "whoever believes in him." He could have also said, "Whoever believes in me"; it is

important that we know "him" in a personal pronoun. None
of the following is Christianity:

Christianity is not a religion — a religion is defined as people seeking God.

Christianity is not a philosophy, a bunch of good ideas.

Christianity is not a set of doctrines.

Christianity is not a church building or a religious organi-
zation or a religious way of thinking.

Christianity is not a list of do's and don'ts.

Christianity is not a spiritual spasm where we say a magical prayer and raise a weepy hand and think that's all there
is to it.

Christianity is our believing in Jesus; it is a relationship with
a personal God — a relationship made possible because of
what Jesus did on the cross for you and for me. Christianity
is a relationship in which we get to go home; we get to return
to the garden and we get to walk once again with our Creator
and our God.

Not simply "believe"

"Whoever believes in him...." Notice that Jesus doesn't say,
"Whoever believes him." Biblical belief, biblical faith and biblical trust are all English words that describe the same concept. Biblical faith is not intellectual assent; it is not believing
Jesus. Biblical faith is not even theism, which is believing that
God exists. In fact, if someone says he is a Christian, he believes Jesus and believes that God exists, one answer is: So
what! The demons believe and they shudder. When the demons see Jesus coming, they know exactly who he is and they
cry out, "O Holy One of God, have you come to torment us?"
Demons are theists; they know God exists. They know who
Jesus is, but they are still going to burn forever in hell.

Biblical faith is not intellectual assent, nor is it theism,
nor is it believing that God will take care of our hurts and
our pains. Biblical faith is not believing that God is going to
change our lives and give us purpose and joy; those are part
of it, but none of these are conversion. Conversion is the experience of those who believe *into* Jesus Christ.

Believe into

This part of the Bible was originally written in Greek; Jesus is going out of his way to use really bad Greek grammar to make the point. In all of recorded Greek literature, no one uses the phrase that Jesus uses here. If you were going to translate it exactly, it would be "that whoever believes into him"; this is horrible Greek grammar, but marvelous theology.

Biblical belief means that we no longer believe in ourselves. Biblical belief means that we no longer trust ourselves. Biblical belief means we have transferred our trust out of ourselves and we have transferred it into Jesus. Biblical belief means that we have made a commitment to trust Jesus, not ourselves. Biblical belief means throwing ourselves into the merciful arms of our loving Creator, fully trusting him for everything: for forgiveness, for salvation, for care, for support, and for all the things that we need as people. Biblical belief means we have thrown ourselves into the merciful arms of God and trust him for everything; and that's a far cry from just believing Jesus.

Psalm 23

One of the best-loved passages in the Bible is in a book called Psalms. In chapter 23 of Psalms, we can see who Jesus is. If we emphasize the pronouns, we can start to get a grasp of what it means to believe into Jesus. The psalmist writes, "The Lord is *my* Shepherd." Think of the relationship that exists between stupid, dumb, smelly, biting, kicking sheep and the Shepherd. "The Lord is *my* Shepherd, *I* shall not want." Here come the pronouns, "*he* makes *me* to lie down in green pastures. *He* leads *me* beside still waters. *He* restores *my* soul. *He* leads *me* in paths of righteousness for *his* name sake. Even though *I* walk through the valley of the shadow of death, *I* will fear no evil" (because I'm a strong, independent being and I can handle whatever life throws at me? No!). "Even though *I* walk through the valley of the shadow of death, *I* will fear no evil for *you*," God, "are with *me*. *Your* rod and staff, *they* comfort *me*. *You* prepare a table before *me* in the presence of *my* enemies. *You* anoint *my* head with oil. *My* cup runs over. Surely goodness and mercy shall follow *me* all the days of *my* life and *I* will dwell in the house," in the presence, "of God forever" (Psalm 23:1-6) .

When we read Psalm 23 that way, we start to get a feel for what this Christianity, this discipleship, this following Jesus is all about. It's understanding that we're stupid, sinful sheep, and we need a shepherd. Our Shepherd not only provides for our forgiveness, but he provides for everything we need: still waters, green pastures, and protection from our enemies. "God so loved the world that he gave his only Son that whoever believes into him" whoever transfers their trust into Jesus (John 3:16).

Salvation is not something we earn

Salvation is not something we earn There is a really important point that I want to emphasize if we are to understand this phrase in John 3:16. If we understand that salvation is not something that we earn, but it's something that God does for us, then it's pretty easy to understand that salvation is not by doing religious things; salvation is by faith. When you and I became disciples of Jesus Christ, we didn't come to him with our hands full of good deeds and say: "Hey, you owe me." "I haven't beaten my wife, lately." "I haven't kicked my dog, lately." "I haven't cheated on my income taxes, lately." "I go to church some of the time, and I even gave a dollar last year."

We don't come to God with things in our hands as if we can earn salvation or earn forgiveness. When we come to understand what salvation is, we understand that it is simply by faith. Salvation is our trusting that when we jump into Jesus' arms, he will catch us and he will save us. The Bible says, "that the wages of sin are death but the free gift of God is eternal life in Christ Jesus our Lord." We are saved and become disciples of Jesus Christ, not by the things that we do as if we were earning favor with God, but by believing that God has done in Christ what we could never do for ourselves.

Paul writes to the Ephesian church, "For by grace you have been saved through faith. And that not of yourselves; it is the gift of God, not as a result of works, lest anyone boast" (Ephesians 2:8-9). There's a song that reads, "Because the sinless Savior died, my sinful soul is counted free, for God the Just is satisfied to look on him" (Jesus) "and pardon me." This songwriter and all true disciples of Jesus Christ understand that we are pardoned not because we have done certain things, but because God through Jesus has done certain things. God the Father, who is loving and just, is content in his mercy to look not on our sin, but to look on Jesus' perfection and to treat us not as we deserve, but to treat us as Jesus deserves. Salvation is nothing that we do for ourselves; salvation is what God has done for us and we respond in faith, believing and trusting that it is so.

Salvation is believing Jesus

The way you and I become disciples or followers or Christians — whatever language you want to use — is not by doing religious things to earn God's favor. You and I become disciples of Jesus Christ by believing that Jesus is who is says he is and by believing that he did what he said he did.

We believe that Jesus is who is says he is. Jesus says, "I am the Way, I am the Truth, I am the Life. No one comes to the Father but by me." We believe that Jesus alone provides forgiveness of sin, and he alone provides access for fellowship and relationship with our Creator. Apart from him, we will die alone for our sin and spend eternity away from his presence in a place called hell. We believe he is who he says he is.

We believe that he has done and will do what he has said he has done and will do. Jesus said, "I did not come to be served, but to serve and to give my life as a ransom for many." We believe that Jesus provided the ransom, the payment, to secure our freedom from sin. We believe that when Jesus cried out, "It is finished," he did complete the work on the cross, and now our sin can be forgiven and we can gain access to our Creator.

Disciples are those who believe Jesus is who he says he is and that he has done what he said he would do.

"MIGHT NOT PERISH BUT HAVE EVERLASTING LIFE"

"For God so loved the world, that he gave his only son that whoever believes in him," not in ourselves, "will not perish but have everlasting life" (John 3:16). If we live our lives separated from our Creator, the only possible option for us is

perishing. Hell is a very real place; we have a taste of it here
and now, don't we? Hell is a real place and all I'm going to
say is this, "you really don't want to go there." Jesus died so
we won't perish, but have everlasting life — eternal life. We
understand that death is a passage into true life lived in full
fellowship with our Creator. The really cool thing about the
gospel is that even before death, you and I get to enjoy some
of the benefits of eternal life here and now. After all, we've
been born again. We have a new Father. We have a new family with new brothers and sisters. We have a new inheritance
waiting for us in heaven. We are aliens now on this cruddy
earth but our citizenship is in heaven.

We live our lives looking forward, longing to go home
and walk in the garden again with God. However, there will
continue to be pain; there will continue to be suffering; there
will be death all around us. Guess what? There will even be
persecution for our new faith. Our friends are not going to
understand why we have changed. We will become, as Paul
says, "The aroma of death to them," but we will also be a
fragrance of life to God. You and I will have new lives with
real joy, the kind of joy that sees past the circumstances of our
lives; it's a true joy that is based in the fact that the emptiness
of our souls has been filled by our Creator. "God so loved the
world that he gave his only Son that whoever believes in him
will not perish but have everlasting life" (John 3:16).

COUNT THE COST

Jesus also says that before we make the decision to believe
into him, we must count the cost because things are never
going to be the same again — they can't be. Salvation is absolutely free and absolutely undeserved; there is nothing that
you can do to earn it. Yet when we make the decision to be
followers of Jesus Christ, it is going to cost us everything because discipleship is discipleship under the Lordship of Jesus Christ. Paul tells us, "you are not your own." Why? The
answer is we were bought with a price, so glorify God and
not ourselves. Glorify God in our bodies. Peter says, "for you
know that it was not with perishable things such as silver or
gold that you were redeemed from the empty way of life, but

rather you were redeemed with the precious blood of Christ."

The blood of Christ is the price God paid to redeem you and me from the pit of hell. Now we who are disciples of Jesus Christ belong to him, and it is a life in which the tyranny of sin has been broken and the mastery of sin over us is gone. Not only do we have lives of freedom and joy, but also lives lived under his Lordship for his glory. Whether we eat or drink, whatever we do, we do to the glory of God. So we have counted the cost and we have joyfully made the decision to follow Jesus.

When we made our decision, God's Holy Spirit came into our lives and he regenerated us, made us into new people and gave us new birth; we were born again. God's Spirit stays within us and he guides and directs us; he even gives us the power to change.

GOD'S GOAL

God's goal for your life and my life is that we change. His will is that we stop looking like what we used to look like, and that we start looking like his Son, Jesus Christ. Paul tells us that we are being changed from one degree of glory to the next, and this is the work of the Holy Spirit in our lives, giving us the desire to change and then the ability to change. The Bible calls these changes the "Fruits of the Spirit."

As God's Spirit is at work inside of us, our lives start to show a kind of love that it's never shown before. Our lives start to understand a deep-seated peace that we've never felt before. We have love, joy, peace, patience, kindness, goodness, faithfulness, gentleness, and self-control because the tyranny of sin has been broken and we are free to serve God; he is at work, giving us these new desires and then the ability to perform them.

What we have done is taken the first steps in new lives of discipleship. God made the world, he loved the world, he gave his Son for the world, and his Son died for the sin of the world, so that those who have placed their trust into Jesus will enjoy the joyous relationship with our Creator now and forever more.

Welcome to the family of God, my brother and my sister.

2

Things Are About to Change

CHANGED PEOPLE

Last time I talked about the fact that after conversion, things are going to change. I also talked about the fact that in conversion, we are born again into a new life — into a new kind of life. My emphasis this morning is on the fact that this new life of the new believer is different; it is, and must be, different from the life lived before conversion. I want to emphasize that we have been changed, and changed people behave in a changed way.

Separation from God

What I'm going to say should not come as a shock to anyone. Think back for a moment to our conversion, and remember what happened in our conversion. We certainly understood that we had been separated from God. We had come to an understanding that we were sinful. We came to an understanding that Jesus' death on the cross paid the penalty for sin so that we could be forgiven. We certainly understood that formerly we did not live in a relationship with God, but after our conversion we did live in a relationship with God, and now he is our Father and we are his children. Even if we just reflect upon these facts, we would say, "Of course my new life as a believer is going to be different; it has to be different because I am different."

Repentance

We certainly understood that in conversion we were called to repent — one of the many ways that Scripture describes conversion. In Acts 3:19-20, Peter is talking to the people and he says, "Repent therefore, and turn again, that your sin may be blotted out, that times of refreshing may come from the presence of the Lord." If we mull over what it means to repent, we will understand that on one hand, it means to change our thinking about who Jesus is and what he has done. In conversion, we changed our thinking from Jesus' being some historical figure to believing that he is God; that is repentance.

Repentance, on the other hand, is not only changing our minds, but it is also the commitment to change our lives and our actions. Repentance is the commitment to turn our backs on sin and turn towards God and live a new kind of life. I think one of the clearest descriptions of repentance is in the book of 1 Thessalonians. Paul had evangelized in Thessalonica probably just four to five months earlier; it was a brand new church, and he had to leave quickly. He wrote these words to the Thessalonian church, so listen to his description to them. "You turned to God from idols to serve the living and the true God" (1 Thessalonians 1:9). This is what repentance is all about: Changing our minds and then making a commitment to change our actions. As we understand the concept of repentance, we're going to say, "Of course my life as a new believer has to be different because I am different."

Dead in sin, alive in Christ

Perhaps in our conversion, we even understood, as in the words of Paul to the church at Ephesus, that prior to our conversion we were dead; we were dead in our sin. However, when we became children of God, he made us alive; marvelous imagery. The fundamental core, the very essence of who we are has been radically and fundamentally changed. We were dead but now we're alive! Certainly, the life of a living person is going to be radically different than the "life" of a dead person. Right? People who are alive tend to have a different set of experiences than people who are dead. Perhaps we understood this concept when we became Christians and now we say, "Of course my new life as a believer is going to be changed, because I was changed; I can't be the same any longer."

So even as we reflect over what we understood as we

became Christians, we're not surprised at all to hear the Bible say that life is going to change for us. Things aren't going to be the same anymore . Perhaps we understood this concept when we became Christians and now we say, "Of course my new life as a believer is going to be changed, because I was changed; I can't be the same any longer." So even as we reflect over what we understood as we became Christians, we're not surprised at all to hear the Bible say that life is going to change for us. Things aren't going to be the same anymore.

WHAT HAPPENED?

As I reflected upon this topic, I started thinking about all the things that happened when I became a disciple of Jesus Christ. In fact, there were many more things that happened to me when I became a Christian at seven years old than a seven-year-old could possibly have understood. I want to help all of our understanding — our picture of conversion — and for some of us, this will be review. Perhaps for some of us, who are new in our faith, our response is going to be, "That happened?" "God did that for me?" "I didn't know that!" "That's amazing!" I want all of you to realize that the more we see and understand the change that God worked in us — whether we fully understood it or not at the time of our conversion — the more we're going to naturally understand that our new lives must be different from our old lives. Our new lives as believers are going to be different because we are different.

Before conversion

Allow me start with what happened before conversion. Did you know that it was God who drew us to himself? Do you understand that when we started, maybe for the first time, to feel guilty or think, "Oh, that wasn't right," then all of the sudden, we started to perceive the need for forgiveness? Yet just the week earlier, we did the same thing and we didn't feel any guilt. Do you know that was God working in us? We were spiritually dead at the time, we couldn't feel guilt. Any dead people feel guilt? No, it doesn't happen. That was God at work in us, drawing us to himself.

When we started to have this sense of emptiness and in-completeness, thinking, "Something's missing in my life," that was not a natural thing, that was God's saying, "I created you for me and I created a vacuum in your heart and I'm the only one that can fill it. Sports can't fill it. Wealth can't fill it. Popularity can't fill it. You can try all you want, nothing can fill it but me."

When we started to understand these things, it wasn't us doing it, but it was God at work drawing us to himself. Jesus says, "No one can come to me unless the Father who sent me draws him."

In fact, when we were finally faced with the claims of Christ and he asked us to believe, do you know that the very faith with which we responded was a gift from God? In Ephe-sians 2:8, Paul tells the church in Ephesus, "For by grace you have been saved, through faith. And that," this entire salva-tion process, "is not of yourselves; it is a gift of God."

So even if we didn't fully understand it, that was God working, pulling, convicting, encouraging, and bringing peo-ple into our lives as he was drawing us to himself.

Responded in faith

Finally, when we were faced with making the decision, and we did respond in faith in our actual conversion — that very moment, we were rescued. We were rescued from the king-dom of darkness and brought into his marvelous kingdom of light; we changed allegiances and our sin was totally forgiv-en. There is nothing we can do to put ourselves out of God's ability to forgive us; that's the power and sufficiency of the cross.

We were *justified*. Justified is a legal term meaning we were acquitted of all our guilt and all our sin; God, the Judge, for-gave us. We were freed from all condemnation, because on the cross, Jesus' death absorbed God's entire wrath against our sin so that we can stand without condemnation; there is no one to condemn us before the Judge.

We were *redeemed*. Redeemed is a term from slavery where Jesus' death on the cross paid the price to secure our freedom, so that we are no longer under the mastery of sin; you and I were redeemed.

We were *sanctified*. We may not always act like it, but we were made holy. Jesus' holiness, his righteousness, was imputed to us; all of that happened when Billy Mounce said, "Yes," and all that happened to you when you said yes to the claims of Christ in your life.

A new creature

Wait, there's more! God caused us to be *born again*. He made us into a *new creation*, new creatures. He *adopted* us as his children. He brought us into a new family with a new Father, brothers, sisters, a new inheritance, and a new home. This world is not our home; my citizenship and your citizenship is in heaven — it's not here. Then God gave us his *Holy Spirit* to encourage us, to guide us, and to guarantee that what Jesus has promised to us will in fact come to pass. You know what? I could go on for pages because the Bible is constantly trying to fill out this picture as it struggles to use language to describe what is indescribable.

The fact is that our lives are going to be different. Our lives can't possibly be the same because we are not the same; that's just the way it is. One of the most powerful passages that describes this is in Romans 6. Paul had to deal with the issue of ongoing sin, breaking God's laws, in the lives of the believers — children of God. In other words, what do we do with disobedient children? In Romans 6:2, he summarizes his answer, "How can we, who died to sin, still live in it?" That's basically what I've been saying. When we consider what happened in conversion and how the language explains that we "died to sin," how can we continue to live in sin? I changed, so therefore, my life must change with it. To explain what he means, Paul goes into a discussion of baptism.

Baptism

We might not be aware of what baptism is, other than seeing the word "Baptist" on the names of some churches around town. Paul goes into a discussion of baptism and its relevance. Allow me to explain

If you are going to be baptized here, we will pull the doors apart behind me and there is a warm hot tub back there. You will go down into the water with me or another pastor or your friend or your mentor who led you to Christ. You will stand in the water and he will ask you to tell your story — your testimony. Then upon profession of faith — upon your saying, "Yes, I believe on the Lord Jesus Christ as my Lord and Savior{ — they will take you put you under the water and then bring you back up; that is baptism.

Understand that baptism is not an act of salvation. Baptism doesn't save anybody. Baptism is an act of obedience; we are commanded to be baptized by Jesus. What we are doing in our baptism is publicly proclaiming that God has changed us. When we are baptized, we are saying, "I believe in Jesus." As we go down under the water, it is not only as if we were being washed from our sin, but it's also as if we were being buried; in other words, we are dying to our old selves. As we are coming up out of the water, it is not only representing again that we have been washed free from our sin (what Christ did for us on the cross), but also that we are coming out to new and different kind of life — changed lives.

I needed to say all of that as background; otherwise, what Paul continues to say in Romans will not make any sense. "Do you not know that all of us who have been baptized into Christ Jesus were baptized into his death? We were buried therefore with him by baptism into death, in order that, just as Christ was raised from the dead by the glory of the Father, we too might walk in newness of life" (Romans 6:3-4). Paul is telling us to think back to our conversions; think back to the public professions in our baptisms. What happened? As we went under the waters, we were dying to our old selves; we were dying with Christ. You and I were somehow mystically joined with Christ, and we died to that old life that we lived. As we come up out of the baptismal waters, we are raised. Just as Christ was raised from the tomb, so also are you and I raised. Just as Christ was raised to a new kind of life, so also you and I come out of our conversion–baptismal experience, being raised to a new kind of life. That is the point that Paul is making in Romans 6.

WHAT DOES THIS NEW LIFE LOOK LIKE?

How can we who died to sin and have been buried with

Christ now live in sin since we have been raised to a new kind of life? If we really understand what happens in conversion and hear the biblical call that our lives must be different, we're going to respond: "Of course my life is going to be different, because I'm different. I've died to sin. How can I live in it?"

So what does this new life look like? What does this newly changed life look like? There are many different descriptions of what a new life look like in Scripture; I'll be hitting on this topic all the way through this series of talks. There are two teachings of Scripture that I want to introduce to you up front to help define what this new life is going to look like.

1. Discipleship

The new life of someone who comes out of conversion is going to be a life of discipleship. When we become Christians, we become followers of Jesus — we become learners of Jesus. We understand that Christianity is not some spiritual spasm; for example, "Oh, yeah, I'm sorry for my sin." Christianity is not a one-time event. We know that conversion is a crucial and necessary step, and it is the first step in a life of being a disciple of Jesus Christ.

One of the most powerful passages along these lines is Mark 8:34, where Jesus says to his disciples, "If you want to follow me, if you want to be a disciple, if you want to be a Christian, you must deny yourself and take up your cross and follow me." Jesus is telling his disciples that if they want to be Christians, if they want to be disciples, if they want to be followers of Jesus Christ, they have to deny themselves. We have to relinquish our wills and submit to the will of God, then everyday we will live as those who have been crucified to their own ambitions and desires and live for the will of God.

Then something happens to us; we get hurt, and our sinful response is, "I have a right to get angry; that person hurt me." Then we hear the words of Jesus' prayer in Gethsemane, "not my will, but yours," God, "be done" (Luke 22:42). So we submit our wills — we relinquish our wills — to God and we forgive the person who hurt us. Or perhaps something unfair happens to us. Our natural response is, "I'm going to get even; that wasn't right. I'm going to teach that person a lesson." Then once again, we hear the words of Jesus, a sinless man crucified, who was treated even more unfairly. He says, "not my will, but yours, be done."

You and I are called to relinquish our wills and to respond with kindness in humility. "Be kind to one another, tenderhearted, forgiving one another, as God in Christ forgave you" (Ephesians 4:32). You see, that's what the life of discipleship is about; it is a life of saying, "This isn't mine any longer, but I live for your pleasure and your glory, God, and it is not my will." We daily, by the minute and sometimes by the second, are called to relinquish our wills and say, "I'm not Bill Mounce; I'm a disciple of Jesus Christ." That's one of the very powerful pictures of what this new life looks like — a life lived in following Jesus.

2. "Fruits of the Spirit"

One of the other pictures that is very powerful is this phrase, "Fruits of the Spirit." I wanted to explain this, but I understand that some of you may not understand any of the words in that phrase. Allow me a little digression and then I'll come back to the phrase. When I talk about the Fruits of the Spirit, or when I even talk about the Spirit with a capital "S," I'm talking about God's Spirit, or someone who is called the Holy Spirit — in older English, the Holy Ghost. How do I explain that? There are a couple of words.

First of all, Christians believe in monotheism. "Mono" meaning "only" or "one," and "theism" meaning "God." We're monotheists — we believe there's *only one God*. The Bible says, "hear, Oh Israel, the Lord our God, the Lord is One." So we're monotheists; we don't believe in multiple gods, we don't believe in local pagan deities, but we believe in one God — his name is Yahweh.

We also believe in a Trinity. We believe in a Trinity not because it makes sense to us, but because the Bible teaches it. "Trinity" is a word that means "three-ness." What the Bible teaches is that while God is one, there are also three "persons" in God: (1) God the Father; (2) God the Son; (3) God the Holy Spirit. Each one is fully God, and each one with a distinct work and a job that he does, and yet there is one God.

We believe this simply because it's the only way to understand the Bible; it's a mystery! I don't even know if we'll fully
understand it when we see him face to face, but we believe
that there is one God and yet he is three.

This third member of the Trinity, this Holy Spirit, is about
whom we're talking when we talk about the Fruits of the
Spirit. The Holy Spirit is who drew us to God. The Holy Spirit
is who enabled us to respond to the Gospel. The Holy Spirit is
who regenerated us and gave us new lives. The Holy Spirit is
who guides us and empowers us every day of our Christian
walk. The Holy Spirit is who gives us the ability to bear fruit;
therefore, we have Fruits of the Spirit. Now we know who the
Spirit is — the third member of the Trinity.

So what does it mean to bear fruit? Just as a healthy fruit
tree produces fruit, a good orange tree produces oranges, and
a good tangerine tree produces tangerines, so also a healthy
Christian's life will change — those changes we call fruit.

Paul writes to the church in Galatia, "But the fruit of the
Spirit," the changes that the Holy Spirit is going to affect in
your life; this is what your life is going to look like, "is love,
joy, peace, patience, kindness, goodness, faithfulness, gentleness, self-control" (Galatians 5:22). All of the sudden, we're
going to realize that while we've always found that certain
person difficult to get along with, now where there was no
love before, or perhaps an imperfect love, we find something
inside of us that wants to put them first; this is called love.

We're going to realize that when things get difficult and
there's conflict or suffering or pain — where in the past we
completely fell apart — now we realize that there's joy in the
midst of the pain! Where did that come from? Not only are
we going to realize there is a joy developing inside of us that
is not based on circumstances, but now there is something
that is down deep that is based in the love and joy of our
relationship with God through Jesus Christ. All of the above
realizations are the Fruits of the Spirit, and this is where our
lives as new believers are headed. The work of God begins
when we start experiencing these kinds of changes.

HOW DO I CHANGE?

We may have already started to see the process of changing. Sometimes change is slower than we like. Sometimes we stumble, but it is a process of changing and growing as we walk as disciples of Jesus Christ, bearing fruit and living changed lives. I think the logical question would be: Is this change automatic? Another way to ask this question is: What is my role in this change or do I even play a role at all? Let me briefly share a few things:

Change is not automatic

First of all, the answer is no; change is not automatic. We can fight change and we can win at our own peril, but the change that God wants to effect in our lives is not automatic. When you and I became Christians, the mastery and the tyranny that sin had over us was broken; we no longer have to sin, but sin is still present and sin is not passive.

One of the lessons I've been learning this year is that for some reason, I had this picture of sin as being passive, lurking around in the recesses of my mind. Sin is not passive, is it? Sin is active, and it is aggressive, and it is going to do everything it can to bring us back to Satan. When you and I became Christians and we were moved out of the kingdom of darkness into the kingdom of light, we made an enemy. He is a formidable enemy and his name is Satan. However, Jesus is greater than Satan is, and he has conquered Satan. Satan did not like losing us from his kingdom and he is going to fight.

God enables us

So change is not automatic, and it's not something that just kind of happens. However, don't get discouraged; we're not going to be able to change on our own. God is not sitting there saying, "Okay, now you have love and you have peace." Somehow, we feel like, "Oh, there are all these things I have to do." No, that's not what's going on. Rather, there is this marvelous, middle position — the biblical position — that says, "God is going to be at work in you, and he is going to be giving you new desires; desires he will give you the ability to accomplish." Then he calls us to cooperate.

I'm not talking about salvation; I did not cooperate with

God in my salvation, because I was dead at the time. I did not do anything to earn God's favor. However, when it comes to areas of Christian growth, God gives us abilities; then through the power of his Spirit, he enables us to move forward and take that next step — but we must take that next step.

There are two strong verses along these lines; one is Philippians 2:12-13. Paul is talking again to the church that is in Philippi. "Work out your own salvation with fear and trembling." In other words, we're not earning your salvation but we're doing the next thing; we're working out the consequences of our conversion. Then he says, "for it is God who works in you"; that's incredible! The God who creates galaxies with distances beyond human comprehension is at work in us. God is at work in us! Then Paul says that God gives us the desire and then the ability to do it. You and I can't do it on our own and God knows that "our frames are but dust," the psalmist says.

But having given us the desire and then the ability, he says in a passage like Romans 12:1,"I appeal to you therefore, brothers, by the mercies of God," because of all that God has done in his mercy, "to present your bodies as a living sacrifice, holy and acceptable to God, which is your spiritual worship. Do not be conformed to this world." What does that mean? As Phillips translates it, "Don't let the world squeeze you into its mold, but be transformed by the renewing of your mind."

So that's the balance of this incredibly new and great Christian walk. God gives us desires. He gives us, through the power of his Spirit, the ability to pursue love, joy, peace, patience, kindness, goodness, faithfulness, gentleness, and self-control. Then he says that we need to take the step. I'm reminded of passages such as Proverbs 3:5-6, "Trust in the Lord with all your heart and lean not on your own understanding, in all your ways acknowledge him." That's what we do, and then the Proverb continues, "and he will make straight your paths." That's God's part. Trust in him. Lean on him. He is our Rock. He is our Refuge. He will direct our paths. He will make our paths straight.

You and I are called to be the salt of the earth. We are called to be different from everyone else. Life has to change because we're different; it's a wonderful walk; it's a joyous walk as we are changed from one degree of glory to the next and look more like our Savior Jesus Christ.

3

When you Stumble

LIVING A CHANGED LIFE

When we became Christians, we changed. We died with Christ to that old life and were raised to a new life — a new life of discipleship; a life in which we submit our wills to the perfect, holy will of God. Our lives started to show the Fruits of the Spirit and we began to have God's love where there was none before; we started to have God's joy and his peace, patience, guidance, goodness, faithfulness, gentleness, and self-control. In other words, our lives changed. Yet this new life of fruitful discipleship isn't automatic, is it?

God is at work in us. He is giving us his desires, and then he is giving us his ability to make those desires a reality in our lives. However, God will not force his desires upon us. He will not make us love. He will not make us be joyous. He will not make us feel peaceful. Rather, we must take the next step. We must agree with God that we want his love, his joy, his peace, and his patience. We must take the next step and, empowered by God's Spirit, be obedient to him. God gives us the desire; he gives us the ability, but we must take the step. For example, the Bible says, "Do not be conformed to this world"; that's a step. "Be transformed by the renewing of your mind"; that also is a step.

Amidst all the joy of our new spiritual lives, I do have some bad news. The bad news is that sometimes, if we're like everyone else, we will fail to take that next step. We will act as if we were not changed in our conversion; instead of love, there will be anger, which might develop into hatred. Instead of joy, there might develop a critical and a bitter spirit. Instead of peace, there could be anxiety and turmoil.

It took me a long time to determine where I was going to raise this topic, because I know all of you are excited. There is so much joy when a person first becomes a child of God. We realize that we are not going to spend eternity in hell; we are going to go to heaven. We realize that we have a new Father and a new family. Yet we need to know that challenges are coming. In fact, those challenges may already have come. So the questions are: "What are you going to do when you haven't taken that next step of obedience?" "What are you going to do when you stumble and fall in the Christian walk?"

DEFINING THREE TERMS

Before I give an answer to the questions above, I need to define three terms that I'm going to use throughout the rest of this talk: relativism, sin and temptation.

Relativism

The first word is not a biblical word. We're not going to find it in the concordance, but it describes the world in which we live, and it describes the culture out of which we have come when we became children of God; that word is "relativism."

Relativism is the denial of the existence of absolute truth; it's the philosophy that there's nothing necessarily right and there's nothing necessarily wrong; it says that truth is relative. Relativism says, "What is true for me may not be true for you. What is true for me this morning may not be true for you this afternoon." Now, the world has a word for this: They call this "post-modern thinking," or "post-modernity." The Bible has a different word for it: It calls it "rebellion" against the authority of God. You and I, as children of God, believe that our Father is the Creator. As the Creator, we believe that he has the right and the wisdom to determine truth. There is absolute truth and it's what God, our Father and Creator, decrees to be truth. In fact, we believe that God himself is Truth. God is the all-wise Creator who determines what is true.

We also believe that God is good all of the time; therefore, this all-wise, all-good Creator wants the best for his creation. This all-wise, all-good Creator gives us rules and guidelines.

He has given us this book, the Bible, and in this book, he has told us what is true and false — what is right and wrong. God has told us what is best for you and for me. At times, we're going to disagree with his judgment call, but truth is not relative; truth is what God has determined. Therefore, what the Bible says is what is best for you and me.

In Psalm 16:11 the psalmist understands this and he says, speaking to God: "you make known to me the path of life; in your presence there is fullness of joy; at your right hand are pleasures forevermore." Notice that the psalmist doesn't write, "Yeah, you gave me a bunch of rules that I have to follow and in your presence I'm just miserable because there's all these things I can't do anymore and there is nothing good about this." That's the sick, weird way people look at Christians and also the way some Christians look at themselves. The psalmist understands that God has made known to us truth — the path of life. Only in his presence is there real joy. Only at his right hand do we find true pleasure.

We are not relativists; we believe there is absolute, moral, spiritual truth. We believe truth is determined not by the world, but by our Creator who is all wise and all good, and he wants the best for his creation. That's the starting point we have and it's diametrically opposed to everything we've been taught in this secular world. We are not relativists.

Sin

The second word I want to define is the word "sin." Sin is a word that we are familiar with, but let me make sure we have a good definition of it. Sin, at its most basic level, is missing the mark. Imagine an archer drawing his bow back and sighting down the arrow. He's sighting for the middle of the target, which is his mark. He lets the arrow fly and the arrow misses the mark; that, at its most basic, fundamental level is what sin is — sin is missing the mark.

Who establishes the mark? Who says this is the middle of the bull's eye? Who says this is where our lives are to aim? God does. Our all-wise, all-good Creator says, "That's the middle." We draw back the arrow of our lives and shoot it, and sin is when the arrow doesn't hit the bull's eye, but it goes aside.

For example, what is God's mark? What is the middle of the bull's eye as far as God is concerned for our tongue? Where is the middle of the bull's eye for our tongue that gets us into so much trouble? He tells us in Ephesians 4:29, "Let no corrupting talk come out of your mouths, but only such as is good for building up, as fits the occasion, that it may give grace to those who hear." 5:4 says, "Let there be no filthiness nor foolish talk nor crude joking, which are out of place, but instead let there be thanksgiving." God has shown us where the middle of the bull's eye is. He is saying, "As far as your tongue is concerned, it is to be so full of grace and thanksgiving, and it is to be so busy building up one another, that there is no room or time to tear the other person down."

We know the middle of the bull's eye, but what happens in our lives? Despite the fact that we truly do believe that God is all wise and all good, there are times when we say things like, "No, God, I know better than you." "Your ways are not always best." "You're not always wise." "This is just not the time to build up, to edify, or to extend grace." So, we gossip, slander, and hurt the other person. We destroy their reputation. We sow seeds of distrust and discontent.

God has shown us the mark and has given us the bull's eye. Sin is when we miss the mark — when we fall short. Sin is simply missing the mark — stumbling in our walk; that is sin.

Temptation

The third word that I wanted to define is the word "temptation." "Temptation" simply means to entice to sin. Someone hurts us, and thoughts go through our head to respond in anger; that's the temptation. Or a woman walks by and — if I believe the statistics now, I have to also say if a man walks by — something inside of us says to look her (or him) up and down; that's temptation; that's the enticement to sin. Let me share with you three things from the Bible about temptation.

1. Temptation is not sin

Temptation is not sin. Thoughts fly through our heads and we say, "Where did that come from?" That is temptation and not sin. Temptation becomes sin when we yield to it, right?

Temptation becomes sin when we yield and we do respond in anger or gossip and slander. Temptation becomes sin when we let our eyes dwell on that woman and we undress her in our minds. Temptation becomes sin when we fall into this fantasy relationship with some guy. Temptation can become sin when we yield to it, but temptation itself is not sin.

2. *You don't have to give in to temptation*

I will show my age, as it will for some of you, when I make mention of a very famous comedian from years ago: Flip Wilson got a lot of laughs with one line. Do you remember his line, "The devil made me do it"? Flip Wilson made a lot of money and got a lot of laughs out of that line, but his theology was absolutely horrific. The devil can't make anybody do anything. Sin can't make us do something wrong.

Understand that on the cross and in our conversion, the mastery of sin was completely broken in our lives. We no longer have to sin; it's still present, but its mastery, its domination, and its control was broken, and we don't have to give in to temptation.

There are promises all the way through the Bible along these lines. Jesus told the disciples in John 16:33, "In the world you will have tribulation. But take heart; I have overcome the world." He conquered the world; he destroyed the absolute power of sin. 1 John 4:4, speaking of God, says that, "he who is in you is greater than he who is in the world."

The God who is in us, through the Holy Spirit, is greater than Satan and anything else this world has. What is inside of us has conquered what is outside of us. Satan simply can't make us sin; we sin because we want to. I sin because I yield to temptation, but never am I made to sin, and neither are you.

The most important promise along these lines is in Paul's letter to the church at Corinth. In 1 Corinthians 10:13, Paul tells them, "No temptation has overtaken you that is not common to man." Here's what is going to happen if we're like everybody else. Temptation is going to come and we're going to feel completely alone; we're going to feel as if no one has ever been tempted like this before — no one has ever had this particular temptation. We're going to feel as if no one had temptation that was this difficult to resist. We may be thinking, "I'm all alone and I'm going to…" (that's Satan, by the way, if you hear that voice). The promise of God is that "no temptation has overtaken you that is not common." We are not alone. No matter how difficult it is, we're not alone. If we are being tempted a certain way, other people are being tempted as well; we are not alone.

Then Paul continues, "God is faithful, and he will not let you be tempted beyond your ability," your ability to resist temptation, "but with the temptation he will also provide the way of escape, that you may be able to endure." Notice that Paul goes not to some inner strength that says, "When you are tempted, just gut it out, hang in there; you can fight it." That's not where he goes. He goes where all good theology goes — he goes initially to the character of God. Paul says that God is faithful. God has made certain promises to us, and our sovereign God is so in control of the circumstances of our lives that he has promised he will never allow a temptation to come into our lives to which we have to yield. We will never have a temptation in which we don't also have some way, by the power of God, to resist. In fact, our all-wise, all-good, all-loving, sovereign God says that in the midst of the temptation there will be a way for us to move through and not yield.

God is not going to keep us away from temptation, but he is going to be with us in the midst of it. As we learn not to yield by the power of his Spirit, we grow in our Christian walk. We never have to sin; we sin because we want to and we like it — I do, anyway. We don't have to sin. We never have to give into temptation. I laughed a lot at Flip Wilson, but he just wasn't right.

3. God is on your side

Please understand that God is on our side. This joy and excitement we are feeling as new Christians is real and there is victory in our walk as Christians; a large part of that is because God is for us, not against us. God wants us to make it — to not yield to temptation.

I had a basketball coach once that needed to read this passage because he wanted me to fail. I've never had a basketball coach like this before, but it was free throws. It was an odd, dysfunctional, triangular relationship between free throws and me and the coach. Every time I got up to shoot a free throw, do you know what I heard? "Miss it!" or "Bet you five bucks you don't make it!" That was my coach! I would hear the coach and the rest of the team say, "Bet you can't make it!" He used to bet me all kinds of things if I missed it. He wasn't a very good coach. I missed a lot of free throws, too, but that is another story. God is not like my basketball coach.

God doesn't want us to fail. He wants us to succeed and not yield to temptation. In fact, he wants us to not yield so badly that he's given of himself to us, and his Spirit lives in us; that's how badly he wants us to win this battle. He's going to give us the desire to win the battle, and then he'll give us the ability to win the battle, too. Paul tells the Galatian church, "Walk by the Spirit and you will not gratify the desires of the flesh." Listen to the Spirit; listen to what he says; listen to the direction that he gives us, and then let his power be the power that helps us not to yield to temptation.

God is on your side. He's on my side. He's not against us; he is for us. Temptation is being enticed to sin; it's not sin in itself, and we don't have to give into it. Understand that we have the power of the risen Christ inside of us to help us not yield to temptation.

WHAT DO YOU DO

Confess

Having discussed those three words, let's get back to the original topic: "What are we going to do when we stumble and sin?" What are we going to do when we miss the mark? I cannot emphasize this enough, because this is one of the defining moments in our spiritual walk. If we don't get this right — if we don't learn what God has called us to do in the midst of sin, we are going to be absolutely miserable for the rest of our lives; I absolutely guarantee it.

The most miserable position in the world is to have a foot in two worlds, and to be hanging onto the world and hanging onto sin. It's just pathetic to see someone, who is a child of God, who possesses the power that raised Christ from the dead — it is the same power that's working in us — hanging onto sin at the same time; this is a defining moment for our spiritual lives. What are we going to do when we stumble and fall? Scripture's answer is very clear: Confess; it's as simple as that. Confess our sin.

All that confession is, is simply agreeing with God that we missed the mark; that's all it is. We say, "God, you are 100% right, and I am 100% wrong. I know the middle of the mark is to have my tongue so filled with grace, understanding and love that there is no room to be critical. I blew it. I'm sorry." That's all that confession is — admitting that you missed the mark, that God's right and you're wrong.

One of the best-known passages is in the book of 1 John 1:8, where John says to Christians, "If we say we have no sin, we deceive ourselves, and the truth is not in us." If anyone thinks they're free from sin, they're deceived, which is what sin is. Right? However, "If we confess our sins, then God is faithful and just to forgive us our sins and to cleanse us from all unrighteousness." Again, John goes to the character of God and says that God is a faithful God — he is a just God. God is committed to forgive our sin if we would but confess.

Psalm 51

If confession of sin is a new thing for you (and it may be for some), I'd encourage you to go to the middle of the Bible, to the book called Psalms, and look at Psalm 51. Psalm 51 is probably the best model of confession that there is anywhere in the Bible. Let me read some of the verses in Psalm 51, and you can start to get a feel for what real biblical confession looks like.

"Have mercy on me, O God, according to your steadfast love. According to your abundant mercy, blot out my transgressions" (Psalm 51:1). Notice that David, the writer, knows that he doesn't deserve to be forgiven, so he appeals to God's mercy.

"Wash me thoroughly from my iniquity. Cleanse me from my sin" (Psalm 51:2). David understands that forgiveness lies ultimately with God.

"For I know my transgressions and my sin is ever before me. Against you and you only have I sinned and done what is evil in your sight" (Psalm 51:3). Although we sin against people, all sin ultimately goes to the heart of God and David knows that.

"Purge me with hyssop and I shall be clean; wash me and I shall be whiter than snow." He knows that forgiveness is fully available.

"Create in me a clean heart, O God, and renew a right spirit within me. Cast me not away from your presence and take not your Holy Spirit from me. Restore to me the joy of your salvation and uphold me with a willing spirit."

Beautiful words! I would encourage each one of you that if you were ever to find yourselves in a situation where you need to confess and the words just don't come, go find a Bible and fall on your knees and crack it open to the middle. Just read Psalm 51 and say, "God, may this be my heart, and may these be my words to you."

As we go through the Psalm, we start to see the principles of confession. We'll see that David makes absolutely no excuses; there are no excuses at all in Psalm 51. There is no idea that he is a victim, but rather it is a complete and total admission of sin by saying, "You're right, God, you're completely right, and I'm completely wrong." David is agreeing with God that sin is really bad. There is no desire in Psalm 51 to minimize sin or to say, "You know, I mean, I've done worse things, and it's not really that bad"; there's none of that in Psalm 51. David agrees that sin is horrific; sin is a wretched thing. Then David calls on God to forgive him; not because he deserves it, because he doesn't, but he calls on God's character of mercy and grace and says, "Because of who you are God, I ask you to forgive me." David knows that he will be forgiven. Psalm 51 is a marvelous model of what real biblical confession looks like, and one against which we need to hold up our understanding of confession and see if our version of confession is or is not biblical.

Tendency to do the opposite

I need to tell you — and it may not happen right now — but as life continues, we will most likely develop a tendency to do the exact opposite of Psalm 51. Again, sorry to be the bearer of bad news, but sin is sin; it's been sin for centuries, and it doesn't change much because it's so effective the way it is. I do know that in my life and in the lives of people that I know, our human tendency (otherwise known as our sinful tendency) is to do the exact opposite of what David does in Psalm 51. Sin is still present in our lives. Its mastery has been broken, but it's still there — nipping, biting, and chomping at our heels because sin knows the power of confession.

Sin knows what confession unleashes in the merciful heart of God, and so it whispers into our ears things like: "No, make excuses." "Don't accept all the blame for what you did." "Certainly you can find someone to blame." "Certainly it's not all your fault." Sin whispers into our ears and the reason it's so effective is that it's coming from the inside, and so we really hear the whispering of sin. Sin whispers, "No, don't fully confess; just confess enough so that you can avoid most of the consequences." These confessions are not deep and gut wrenching such as: "God, against you I have sinned." "I am wretched in my sin." "I cannot believe that you will forgive me, but I do believe that you will forgive me." "I am so, so sorry." How many times on our lips has there been that kind of confession? So often, confession is just enough so that we can avoid the consequences of our sin, and of course, none of this is true confession; none of this brings full forgiveness, and none of this brings cleansing. Only a Psalm 51 kind of confession brings full cleansing.

PRACTICAL SUGGESTIONS

Allow me to give a couple of practical suggestions when it comes to confession of sin.

Get it over with

The tendency I have, and I think most people have, is to mull it over for awhile — to think whether it is really that bad. Just get it over with. Confess it early. Confess it often. Confess it fully. Just get it over with! As you or I hold onto our sin, what we're doing is only hurting ourselves, we are only falling farther down the spiral of sin, and we are only damaging our relationship with God, and the walls are going up.

The thing about confession that is also important is that

when you and I confess, we're not telling God something he doesn't already know; it's not like we're going to hang onto this deep, dark secret, and we're not going to tell God! Just get it over with. Confess early. Confess often. Confess fully. God sees what goes on at 1:00 in the morning. God hears what we whisper. He knows exactly what is going on in our lives and in our hearts; we're not keeping anything from him — we're not telling him anything he doesn't already know. You and I are the ones who are being hurt when we refuse to confess our sin.

Confess your sin to one another

A second piece of practical advice is to simply confess our sin to one another; this is not just a good idea, this is the Bible (James 5:16). Part of the lie of sin is that while we're in the darkness of sin and we think no one else knows that we're fighting with this sin, sin will tell us things such as: "Don't tell anybody." "It will only get worse if you tell anyone." "No, just keep this to yourself and work with it." "If you told another Christian, you're giving them power over you — giving them authority. You don't want that! They'll gossip about you and it's only going to get worse." Have any of you heard that voice? It's the voice of Satan; it's the voice of sin; it's the voice of the lie.

The fact of the matter is that the power of sin is snapped when we bring it to the light. If we were in a different environment and we were all being honest, we could probably all tell stories of times in which the sin was yanking at us and pulling us down, taking us farther and farther down that spiral. Then we start to get desperate, wondering how we are ever going to get out of this sin. In obedience to Scripture and perhaps in desperation, we finally to go to someone we trust and confess to them saying, "I need you to pray for me."

What happens when we do that? It's over. It's amazing how the power of sin is snapped when we bring it to the light. Right? Right! Get it over with and confess our sin to one another. Sin is always going to be here. Sin never goes away until we die and go home. Part of the Christian walk is learning to deal with sin. In the midst of our sin and our confession, we are being changed from one degree of glory to another so that we look more and more like Jesus Christ. That's what this is all about, right?

RECEIVE HIS FORGIVENESS

What happens when we confess? We receive his forgiveness. I John 1:9, "If we confess our sins," because of his very character of being a faithful and a just God, he absolutely commits himself, "to forgive us our sin and to cleanse us from all unrighteousness." Perhaps as our Christian walk develops, we may get caught in sin and we'll ask, "How could God love a sinner like me?" The answer is that he loved us before conversion; why would he not love us now? He loved us when we weren't his children; why would he stop loving us now that we are his children?

The thought may go through our minds, "But how could God really love someone who keeps on doing the same things over and over again? How can he really forgive me?" The answer: because he's God, and that's what being God is about. I would struggle if you kept sinning, and even though I know the Bible says I have to keep forgiving you seventy times seven — just keep forgiving — it's hard because I'm human. God isn't human; he's God and he's a faithful God. God is committed no matter how much we sin, or how many times we commit the same sin, or no matter how bad it gets. If we confess our sin and say, "God, you're right, I'm wrong," he will commit himself, always, with no exception, to forgive us our sin and to cleanse us from all unrighteousness.

BE CLEANSED

If you want to know what it's like to be cleansed, go to Psalm 103; this is another one of those model Psalms on confession. If you're caught in sin and want to be forgiven and can't find the words, find Psalm 103. Read it as your own words. I'm going to start at verse 8.

"The Lord is merciful and gracious, slow to anger and abounding in steadfast love. He will not always chide, nor will he keep his anger forever. He does not deal with us according to our sins, nor repay us according to our iniquities. For as high as the heavens are above the earth, so great is his steadfast love toward those," who are his children, "who fear him; as far as the east is from the west, so far does he remove our transgressions from us. As a father shows compassion to his children, so the Lord shows compassion to those who fear him. For he knows our frame; he remembers that we are dust."

That's God's cleansing method! God has determined what is true and false, what is right and wrong, and what is good and bad. He is our all-good, all-wise Creator, who wants his best for his creation. With all of the joy and all of the victory that there is in the Christian walk, there's also sin; there's stumbling and falling; there's yielding to temptation and missing the mark. Please, confess your sin. Confess early. Confess often. Confess fully. Tell God, "You are absolutely right and I am absolutely wrong. No one else is to blame. I messed up. I'm sorry. Please forgive me." God is committed to forgive, and we will enjoy the freedom that comes from being forgiven and cleansed.

PSALM 32

I want to leave each of you with one last Psalm. Another model Psalm for confession is Psalm 32. Starting in verse 3 the psalmist describes what it was like not to confess sin. He says, "For when I kept silent," when I did not confess my sin to God, "my bones wasted away through my groaning all day long. For day and night your hand was heavy upon me; my strength was dried up as by the heat of summer." In another Psalm he talks about his tongue sticking to the roof of his mouth.

However, what happens when he does confess his sin? Verse 5, "I acknowledged my sin to you, and I did not cover my iniquity; I said, 'I will confess my transgressions to the Lord,' and you forgave the iniquity of my sin." Then back to verse 1,"Blessed is the one whose transgression is forgiven, whose sin is covered. Blessed is the man against whom the Lord counts no iniquity, and in whose spirit there is no deceit."

4

Listening to God

When you and I became a Christian, we entered into a new relationship. And one of the crucial elements of any relationship is communication, both speaking and listening. And since we "always" listen before we talk, I want to talk today about listening to God.

REVELATION

There are three terms I want to make sure we understand as we talk about what it is to listen to God. The first is "revelation." Revelation is simply God making himself known to us. Revelation is God speaking so that we can listen to him. And God speaks to us and we hear him in two basic ways.

1. General Revelation

One way we call general revelation, which is information about God that is available to all people of all time. This is God speaking to all people and all people being able to hear what he has to say. In Romans chapter 1, Paul has been talking about the fact of people's sin and their responsibility for their sin. It's within this context beginning in verse 19 that Paul says this. "For what can be known about God is plain to them because God has shown it to them. For his invisible attributes, namely his eternal power and divine nature, have been clearly perceived ever since the creation of the world in the things that have been made." Paul is saying that in creation, God is clearly, plainly speaking. And everyone who has ever lived, regardless of time and place, is able to hear this particular voice of God. There are three things that God has been saying. The first is implicitly, that "I exist." Secondly, he has been telling everyone about his power. And thirdly, he's been telling everyone about his divinity. Divinity simply means that he is separate from creation, that creation does not hold the key to its own existence, but that the Creator of creation lies outside of creation. And Paul is saying that in creation, God has been speaking this, proclaiming this to all people and all people should have been able to hear that.

This is the same theme that the psalmist picks up in Psalm 19. This psalm is really a celebration of God's revelation. Starting at verse 1, the psalmist writes, "The heavens declare the glory of God and the sky proclaims his handiwork. Day after day pours out speech and night after night reveals knowledge. There is no speech nor are there words whose voice is not heard. Their voice goes out through all the earth and their words to the end of the world." In creation itself, God is speaking and he is proclaiming his existence and his power and his divinity — those invisible attributes of God.

Certainly, as we think about listening to God, we have to learn to listen, to pay attention to his voice in creation, don't we? It's one thing to go out and stand on the Oregon coast and say, "That's beautiful." But what we have to do is to say, "It is beautiful because a beautiful God created this." And as we see the sunset over those large beaches, we think of God. And that is what those beaches are doing. The beaches are declaring the glory of God.

We look at pictures of galaxies — one of my favorite things to look at — and we see the distance and the brightness and the power, but what we need to see more than anything else is the awesome power of the Creator God who made millions of galaxies. As we look close-up at pictures of flowers, and we see the intricacies and the delicacies and the beauty of a flower, we think of the God who is separate from the flower and yet proclaims himself to us through the flower.

This is us learning to respond and learning to hear what God is saying generally through his creation and it is clear. It is clear and it is profound.

Yet, you could stand as long as you wanted on the Oregon coast and you're never going to hear God saying, "My Son died on the cross for your sins." General revelation doesn't have the capability of teaching us that salvation is by grace through faith, for example. For that, we need the other kind of revelation. And we call that specific revelation.

2. Specific Revelation

Specific revelation is information about God that is available only to some people, some of the time. Specific revelation is when God is speaking to only certain people who are capable of hearing what he says. Specific or "special" revelation is the technical name for what we also call the Bible. The Bible goes by many names — Scripture, the Word, the Word of God — but it is this that contains special, specific revelation and this is how we hear God speak to us, even if other people in other places of other times were not able to hear the same thing.

If you continue in Psalm 19, he goes through a few more verses and he talks more about creation declaring things about God, and then in verse 7, he switches to the specific revelation and he says, "The law of the Lord is perfect, reviving the soul" — the "law of the Lord" is another name for the Bible. "The testimony of the Lord is sure, making wise the simple. The precepts of the Lord are right, rejoicing the heart. The commandment of the Lord is pure, enlightening the eyes." Down to verse 10: "More to be desired are they than gold, even much fine gold; sweeter also than honey and drippings from the honey comb. Moreover, by them is your servant warned. In keeping them there is great reward." Psalm 19 is the celebration of the fact that God has chosen to speak to us so that we can actually hear him. We can hear of his existence and his power and his divinity as he speaks through creation, but we can learn so much more as he speaks to us through his special revelation, the Bible.

THE BIBLE

In a half hour, I have to pick and choose what I want to share with you about the Bible, and there's a lot more that could be said. But the one thing I have been wanting to say, which has been a little frustrating up to this point, is basically how we reference the Bible, how we get around in it and refer to pieces of it.

The Bible is basically divided into two parts and we call

them the Old Testament and the New Testament. Each of
those testaments is broken into books. There are 39 books in
the Old Testament and 27 books in the New Testament.

I want to encourage you sometime to open your Bible and,
if you're not familiar with it, to thumb through the Table of
Contents to get used to the names of the books, so if I say "2
Timothy" you'll think, "Oh, that's a book in the Bible."

The Testaments are broken into books and the books, then,
are broken into chapters and chapters are broken into verses.
The way we reference a place in Scripture is to say, for example, "In John 3:16…" and what that means is that John is the
name of the book, which happens to be in the New Testament, 3 is the chapter, and 16 is the verse. So, I haven't been
able to reference Bible verses to you earlier, but now I can.
John 3:16 — book, chapter, and verse.

There's also a handout that you have and I would encourage you to go through it and spend some time with it. It's
the names of all the books in the Bible broken into general
categories and it will kind of give you a feel for what's in the
Bible and where, so you just need to spend some time going
through that.

FOUR IMPORTANT TOPICS

There are four topics that I can't really talk about the Bible
without mentioning and, again, I'm not going to have the
time to go into them in detail but I do want to mention con-
clusions about these four different topics/terms. If these are
concepts that are important to you, I'd encourage you to go
to BiblicalTraining.org and go to the section *Foundations*, and
several of the lectures in the class *Why I Trust My Bible* are going to be my discussion of these four words that I just want to
share with you very briefly in talking about the Bible.

1. Inspiration

We believe in the inspiration of the Bible. We believe that the
Bible is inspired. What that basically means is that we believe
the Bible comes from the very mouth of God. Inspiration is
a doctrine that is primarily concerned with source and so if
you go to the book of 2 Timothy 3:16, you can see Paul write,

"For all of Scripture is inspired." Some of the newer translations say, "All of Scripture is breathed out by God." Actually, Paul makes up a word, which is why it's hard to translate it. He takes the word for "God" and he takes the word for "breathed" and — you can do this in Greek — he just sticks them together and he says, "You figure out what it means." All of Scripture is God-breathed.

All of Scripture, we believe, comes from the very mouth of God. In another book called 2 Peter, in chapter 1 starting in verse 20, Peter says this about Scripture: "No prophecy of Scripture comes from someone's own interpretation, for no prophecy was ever produced by the will of man but men spoke from God" — there's the origin — "as they were carried along by the Holy Spirit." When we talk about the inspiration of the Bible, what we believe is that different men sat down and wrote these words, but they were carried by the Holy Spirit. In other words, the Holy Spirit controlled what they were writing such that what they wrote were the very words of God. That's the doctrine of inspiration.

2. Authority

We believe in the authority of Scripture. If you continue to read in 2 Timothy 3:16, it says, "For all Scripture is breathed out by God and is [therefore] profitable for teaching, for reproof, for correction, and for training in righteousness." And what Paul is telling Timothy is that if you understand the source of Scripture, that it comes from the very mouth of God, it therefore comes with his authority. So when you go to teach or correct or reprove or train someone, you don't use human words and human wisdom. You use God's Word.

So the doctrine of inspiration is that Scripture comes from God and because it comes from God, it bears God's authority. I don't preach out of this book because it's magical. I preach out of this book and we believe the book because we believe the words come from God and, therefore, his words come with his authority. So, my job is to proclaim what God has said and not what I think. So the doctrines of inspiration and authority are tied together very, very closely. Please understand that the Bible does not share its authority with anything or anyone because God does not share his authority with anything or anyone.

This book is not in competition with the Koran. This book is not in competition with the writings of Joseph Smith. This book is not in competition with human philosophy. This book is not in competition with church tradition and the edicts of popes and the statements of priests. This book does not compete with anyone for authority because God does not compete with anyone for authority. Scripture and Scripture alone is our source of authority and our source of truth and our source of guidance, and it is to this that we go, not because it's magical or you can buy it in any color and put funny colors on the edge. We go to it because we believe it comes from the very mouth of God.

3. Canonicity

The third thing I wanted to mention is the issue of canonicity. It's a fabulous topic and there are many books and different lectures you can listen to if you want to learn more about it. Canonicity is simply the process by which the Holy Spirit worked through the Church as a whole in helping the Church understand which books are truly inspired. There were a lot more books than 66 written and, through the power of the Spirit, we believe that he guided the early Church as a whole in identifying these 66 as truly being from God and all the other ones that people nowadays keep holding up and saying, "You really should be reading the Gospel of Thomas" — we believe that they're wrong because God controlled the Church in the process of canonicity.

By the way, if anybody says to you that the Gospel of Thomas should be in the Bible, ask them if they've read it. All you have to do is read the Gospel of Thomas and you can understand that it can't possibly be Scripture. It's nothing like the Bible and it was written in AD 180 so Thomas didn't write it unless he was really old, and he wasn't.

4. Trustworthy

The fourth thing I wanted to mention is that we believe the Bible is trustworthy. Because it comes from God, it not only has our allegiance, but we believe that the writers got it right. When they say that "Jesus did this" or "Jesus said this," we believe that, guided again by the Holy Spirit — which is one of Jesus' promises to them that "the Holy Spirit will come and cause you to remember everything I have taught you" — we believe that's exactly what happened. Therefore, this is a faithful witness to what Jesus taught in the Gospels and this is a faithful witness to the growth of the early Church and what the apostles taught.

Again, I know it's very popular in some circles to say, "Oh, I can't believe the Bible. It's not trustworthy. It's so full of contradictions." One way to deal with this is simply to ask, "Really? It's full of errors? Can you show me one."

"It's just so full of errors, I mean, they're all over the place."

You reply, "If it's so full of errors, then you should be able to point one out to me quite easily."

The fact of the matter is that most don't know where the problems are. They just don't want to trust it. We believe the Bible is trustworthy, that it doesn't contradict itself. So, I just can't talk about the Bible without mentioning those four things: inspiration of Scripture; the authority that comes from God's Word; the fact that the early Church, by the power of God's Spirit, got the right 66 books; and that it's absolutely trustworthy, that when the Old Testament prophets say, "Thus saith the Lord," that the words that came out and the words that are written down truly came from the mouth of God.

WHAT DO YOU DO WITH THE BIBLE?

What I wanted to emphasize today is the whole question of what do you do with this? What do you do with this book? It's all fine and good to argue about inspiration and authority and canonicity and trustworthiness — some of us love to argue about these things. But the question is, is that what this is here for? The answer is obviously no. So, the question is, what do we do with this book? Let me encourage you to do four different things with it.

1. Read it!

Some of us love to read. We love to read all kinds of things. We love to read about the Bible. We love to read people's understanding of the Bible. We love to read biographies about how the Bible has impacted people's lives. But, do we love to read the very words of God? It's so easy to be caught up in reading things about it, but do we read the words of God? Let me encourage you to read it for at least three different reasons.

First, healthy relationships require healthy communication. It's kind of one of those "no, duh" kind of statements but it is true. Healthy relationships require healthy communication and if we are going to have a healthy relationship with our Redeemer, then we have to communicate. We communicate partially by listening to him, and we listen to him by reading what he has said. This is a common sense thing about healthy relationships and, like any relationship, I would encourage you to listen to your Redeemer regularly and listen to your Redeemer often.

The favorite time of day for me is the first hour of every morning. My wife, Robin, and I, after a few years of trying different things, developed a ritual where we get up early and the kids aren't up yet and there's no noise. Nothing major has gone wrong … yet. It's still quiet, reasonably peaceful, and after four cups of coffee we're ready to talk. We have about an hour together and it's a wonderful quiet time. We say things like, "How'd you sleep? How do you feel? What are you doing today?" Healthy communication. "What's God teaching you? What did you read last night that really made a difference in your life that perhaps you've been mulling over this morning?" That's healthy communication. It's regular, it's every morning, it's frequent.

The same thing that is true in our marriage is true in our marriage with our God, because we are his Bride. Men and women alike, we are the Bride of Christ. And we must communicate with him if we are to have a healthy relationship with him. You may have heard the phrase "quiet time." This is what quiet times are all about; you and I need to fine some place to get away on a regular basis and do it often, where it's quiet, it's peaceful, and we can listen to God and then we can speak with God. Healthy relationships need healthy communication. That means we have to set times aside to listen to him.

Secondly, I want to emphasize that if we don't read it, how will we know what God is saying to us? If we don't read it, how will we know what is truly best? If we don't read it, how will we really know what is true? If you're not "in the Word," as the expression goes, if you're not reading this book, the Bible, how will you know what the very, very, very, very, very most important thing to do every day is? Terrible grammar, but you get the idea. What is the most important thing? What is the greatest commandment that God has for us? To go to church? That's not what it says! "To love the Lord your God with all your heart, and all your soul, and all your mind, and all your strength." If you do nothing else but you do that, then you've done the most important thing.

But you're not going to know that if you haven't been reading. You're not going to know that we're into cloning. Christians are the primary cloners of the universe, because disciples are to replicate themselves. But you're not going to know that if you haven't read the Great Commission. Jesus says, "Go make disciples." That's what we're here for, to make disciples, baptizing them in the name of the Father and the Son and the Holy Spirit. Every one of us is to be involved in evangelism one way or another. Then all of us are to be involved in making fully-devoted disciples, "teaching them to obey absolutely everything that I've taught you," Jesus said.

These are things that you don't know if you don't spend time reading. So, I encourage you that if you want to know what our all-wise, all-good God is holding out to you and saying, "this is the best, this is the truth" — you won't know it unless you listen to him and you can't hear him unless you read him.

Thirdly, I want to mention that you need to ask the Holy Spirit to help you understand. As you read it, he is your best Teacher. He's better than your preacher. He's better than your Sunday school teacher. And he's better than all those books that you might want to read about the Bible. The Holy Spirit is your best Teacher.

Paul tells the Corinthian church that the god of this world has blinded the minds of unbelievers. Before you became a Christian, Satan blinded your eyes and those blinders have now been taken off. But you have a ways to go — I have a ways to go — and we go that way by asking the Spirit to help us understand what God our Father is saying to us.

In the book of 2 Corinthians chapter 2, Paul says this starting at verse 12: "Now we have received not the spirit of the world, but the Spirit who is from God that we might understand the things freely given us by God. And we impart this in words not taught by human wisdom but taught by the Spirit, interpreting spiritual truths to those who are spiritual."

Let's covenant to be a people of the Book. It's not a hoop to jump through. It's not a ritual to earn favor with God. It's none of those things. It's just common sense. We've entered a new relationship. If we want a healthy relationship, we need to communicate. Part of communication is listening and so we listen by reading.

2. Meditate on it!

Secondly, let me encourage you to meditate on the Bible. There are many mornings in which I'm talking with Robin where she'll say things to me, and they just won't click. They don't make sense to me. But she's usually right and I'm usually wrong, so when things don't click it's usually my fault. What I need sometimes is time to mull it over.

Robin loves to read dead people. If you want to know where my illustrations come from, if the person is over 100 years old, it's Robin giving me those illustrations. She loves to read people who are dead. It's a good way to read good stuff. She'll give me these illustrations. She'll talk about things that the Church was talking about in 1850. It takes me a while to mull over some of this stuff and think through it. But I'm so committed to our relationship and I trust her so much that I'm committed to meditating on her words. I'm committed to mulling it over and thinking and, even if it didn't make a lot of sense to me at first, I'm committed to giving her the benefit of the doubt. That's what meditation is.

Now, some of you may have red flags that go up when I say "meditation" and you may be thinking of Eastern religious meditation. That is not what I'm talking about. The kind of meditation that we see coming out of the Far East is wrong because they teach you to open your mind. That's their meditation. All you have to do is talk to someone who's been a Satanist and he will tell you that there's nothing Satan loves more than Christian kids meditating and "opening their minds," because Satan will head straight for that empty vacuum. Christian meditation is the exact opposite. It is filling your mind with the things of God. It's filling your mind with the things of Scripture, mulling over, thinking, giving it the benefit of the doubt because you know that ultimately, it's right.

So you work on it, and you listen to it, and you mull, and you meditate. It takes work but it's worth the effort. A relationship with God is worth the effort to mull over and to think. So whether you're driving to work or you're on a coffee break or it's lunch or the computer's blurring before your eyes and you need a ten-minute break — stop and meditate. Stop and fill your mind with what you've been reading in Scripture. Repeat the verse that you've been memorizing and ask God to make sure you understand it and can apply it in your life.

If you do that, do you know what Scripture promises? It promises that you'll be blessed. I don't know about you, but I like being blessed by God. Psalm 1 says, "Blessed is the man who walks not in the counsel of the wicked, nor stands in the way of sinners, nor sits in the seat of scoffers." Blessed is the person who stays away from sinners. "But his delight is in the law of the Lord and on his law he meditates" — on Scripture, he meditates — "day and night." And here's what a blessed man looks like: "he is like a tree planted by streams of water that yields its fruits in its season and its leaf does not whither." That's God's blessing, that you and I are this tree planted by the streams of life that flow from him and flow through his holy Word. As we draw nourishment from that stream, we grow and we become oaks of righteousness. But you can't get there just by reading. It requires meditation, mulling, reflecting.

3. Memorize it!

Thirdly, let me encourage you to memorize it. "Oh no, I can't memorize anything since poetry in fifth grade!" Let me encourage you as I've been encouraging myself to memorize Scripture. It's worth the effort. It's worth it to have God's truth on the tip of your tongue. It's worth it when your mind is so saturated with the words of God that no matter what happens, we know what is true and we have a pretty good idea how to respond in a situation.

The psalmist says, "I have stored up your Word in my heart, that I might not sin against you." How will we know what sin is unless we have stored up Scripture in our minds and memorized it? And so we memorize Scripture. We memorize verses, perhaps paragraphs, perhaps chapters, so that when we face temptation, we recall the story of how Jesus responded when he faced temptation. He responded the same way all three times, didn't he? He quoted Scripture. But even more, when we face temptation and temptation is saying, "Oh, go ahead and do that. It's kind of dangerous but you can test God and he's promised to take care of you," the verse goes through our head, "You shall not test the Lord your God," because we've memorized Jesus' response to Satan.

Or perhaps life is difficult and the pressures are weighing on us, and the thought goes through our head, "hey, if this is what Christianity is about, I don't want anything to do with this. It isn't any fun and it's too difficult," and the verse is floating through your head where Jesus says, "Take my yoke upon you and learn from me. I am gentle and lowly in heart and you will find rest for your souls. For my yoke is easy, and my burden is light." And that verse floats through our head and we say, "If Jesus promised that his yoke is easy and his burden is light, then why am I under such oppression?" And the verse helps.

Loneliness is at an epic and all-time high in Western culture. We are so connected but most of it is false connection and there's not the deep intimacy that we crave. Americans, especially, are phenomenally lonely. So you're in a situation and the loneliness is intense, and the last words of Jesus to his disciples in the Gospel of Matthew float through your head: "I am with you always, even to the end of the age."

This is the beauty of memorization where these verses are on the tip of our tongue and our minds are saturated with the very words of God, that when we get in a situation, there's the answer, there's the truth, there's the stuff to help.

I've noticed that approximations really don't help. Have

you noticed that? I heard of an incident last night — it wasn't my daughter — where someone's daughter was stuck in Albany and the airlines seemed to have no concern whatsoever that she couldn't get on the airplane. There was the tendency to be anxious and the verse floats through our head, "Be anxious about nothing, but by prayer and supplication, make your requests known to God." And the verse that Paul gives the Philippians also goes through our mind: "And the peace of God that passes all understanding will keep your hearts and minds in Christ Jesus." It's one thing to have your daughter stuck in Albany and say, "OK, God, I'm getting anxious here. Um, OK, what's that verse? Uh, God promised me peace, um, but what about peace?" It just doesn't work, does it? But we're to "be anxious about nothing, but by prayer and supplication, make your requests known to God. And the peace that passes all understanding will keep your hearts and minds in Christ Jesus." See, that's the power of memory. And I would encourage you as I'm beginning more and more to encourage myself to commit Scripture to memory, so it's there on the tip of my tongue, saturated in my mind.

4. Obey it!

Fourthly, let me encourage you to obey it. Sometimes we get this feeling that all I have to do is know it, but I don't have to really do it. I can quote verses about not being anxious but what happens when the temptation comes to be anxious? Let me encourage you not just to read it or meditate on it or memorize it, but we must obey it. When you know Scripture but you don't obey it, there's a word for that. It's called "being a fool."

The end of the most famous sermon in the world, the Sermon on the Mount, Jesus says, "The person who hears my words and does them is like a man who built his house on a rock, and the storms of life come and the house stands firm. But whoever hears my words and does not do them is like a foolish man who built his house on the sand. And the storms come and the wind comes and the rain comes and great is the destruction of that house." It doesn't do any good to know it if we don't obey it and put it into practice.

You know what's going to happen as you and I read it and

learn it and obey it? We start to trust it.

The world has a lot of truth claims out there. There are a lot of things the world is saying are true and it's over there and Scripture is over here and we have to choose. Are we going to believe the world or are we going to believe God? This is just a process we all go through. I was watching "60 Minutes" a while back and I was told that it is unreasonable to think that any human being could control his or her sexual urges. And the person described us as dogs. You can't expect a dog to control its sexual behavior; well, you certainly can't expect our teenagers to. That's what the world says.

And over here, Scripture makes another truth claim and it says, "But among you, there must not even be a hint of sexual immorality, or of any kind of impurity, or of greed because these are improper for God's holy people." And you look at that and think, "Who do I believe? I know I'm supposed to believe this, but everything in me is telling me to believe that over there." And we have to make this choice. Sometimes we choose the world and we tell God he doesn't know what he's talking about. And other times, even when it doesn't make any sense to us, we choose to believe God. Has God ever been wrong? The answer is no, never. Even in those situations — I've noticed this in my life — even when I've read some things in Scripture and I think, "you know, if that wasn't God saying that, there's no way I'd ever believe it because that's the silliest thing I've ever heard." "Don't let any foolish laughter come out of your mouth?" That's stupid. But as we make this faith choice and as we choose to obey, we find out that he's always true. He's always right. And that builds trust.

As we obey and as we grow in our trust, then we start to be transformed and that's the ultimate goal of all this. Paul tells the Corinthian church that "we, by beholding the glory of God, are being transformed into the same image, the image of his Son, from one degree of glory to the next." As we obey it, and as we grow in our trust of it, we start to be transformed because we start to look more and more like Jesus. May that be true of all of us. May we become people of the Book.

5

Speaking with God

When we became Christians, we entered into a relationship with our Creator. Like any relationship, communication plays a major role. God speaks to us and we listen to him as he speaks to us primarily through Scripture. God also listens to us as we speak with him in prayer. Our listening to and speaking with God is prayer. Prayer is listening to God and speaking with God, talking to him about anything and everything; it's a joyous time, it's a privilege, and it should be absolutely natural for his children.

HOW DO I PRAY?

As new Christians, we may be asking, "Okay, how exactly do I pray?" Jesus' disciples asked the same question and Jesus' answer is known as the Lord's Prayer; it is in the Gospel of Matthew, the first book of the New Testament. In Matthew 6:9-13, Jesus teaches us how to pray; I want to spend my time this morning on this passage.

Notice how Jesus starts, "Pray then, like this." Jesus did not intend this model prayer to be mindlessly repeated as if it were some kind of magical incantation. He never intended the Lord's Prayer to be something we would be saying in church while we're thinking of something else. The Lord's Prayer is intended to give us the basic structure and the basic content of what prayers in general should look like. I think there is quite a bit of room for flexibility as we pray through the Lord's Prayer, but we are supposed to pray "like this."

"OUR FATHER IN HEAVEN"

Jesus starts, "Our Father in heaven." Prayer starts with a proper view of God. Prayer starts with our understanding of who God is and what he is like.

He is our Father. When Jesus was speaking, he would have been speaking in Aramaic. The Aramaic word for father is Abba; you may have heard that word-it's not just a Swedish pop-music group! Abba was the word that a child would use to address his or her father, and it is a term of familiarity.

By starting prayer with "Our Father," Jesus is teaching us to approach God with that sense of familiarity — that sense of family. He wants us to understand that the God to whom we are praying, the God with whom we are speaking, cares for us in the same way that a father cares for his children. He is also our Father "in heaven." Jesus is teaching us that we can never forget that "Our Father," with whom we are talking, is also the God who has created all things, who sustains all things, and who merely spoke and galaxies came into existence. He is teaching us to approach God with astonishment and trembling and reverence and awe.

So Jesus teaches us to start our prayers, "Our Father in heaven." He is teaching us to pray with this mix of familiarity and reverence.

FOCUS FIRST AND FOREMOST ON GOD

Jesus then moves into the prayer. In the first half of the prayer, we can see that prayer focuses first and foremost on God, not us.

It's not going to be clear in most translations, but the Lord's Prayer is made up of a series of imperatives. In the Lord's Prayer, we are calling on God to act, but we are not calling him to act primarily on our behalf. We're calling him to act primarily on his behalf. In our prayer, we are calling on God to act in such a way that his glory be spread abroad. We are calling on God to act in such a way that people will praise and honor him, not us.

"Hallowed be your name"

The first of those imperatives is "Hallowed be your name," or more accurately it should be translated, "May your name be hallowed." "Hallowed" is an old word that we like to hang onto in the church and it simply means holy or sinless. When we pray, "May your name be hallowed," it's not that we're making God something that he isn't. What we are saying is that we are calling on God, as an imperative, to act in such a way that people see that he is holy. We are calling on God to act in such a way that people see that he is glorious, sinless, and perfect in all of his attributes. "Through what you do, God, may your name be seen to be what it truly is: holy, perfect, sinless, glorious. In all that we say and don't say, in all that we do and don't do, may people see that you are, indeed, a holy God." That's what we're saying when we say, "hallowed be your name."

"Your kingdom come"

The second imperative is "Your kingdom come," or more properly, "May your kingdom come." God's kingdom is not some earthly realm. Jesus took care of this with Pontius Pilate when he said, "If my kingdom were of the world, my followers would have fought for it. My kingdom's not of this world."

God's kingdom is his kingly rule in the hearts and lives of his children. When you and I pray, "May your kingdom come," what we are praying is, "God, will you exercise your kingly rule in me, such that it spreads out through me to all of those with whom I come into contact. May your kingdom spread through what I say and don't say. May your kingdom spread through what I do and don't do."

At the end of time, when God has had his fill and he sends Jesus back, as Paul tells the Philippian Church, then, "every knee will bow and every tongue will confess that Jesus Christ is Lord to the glory of God the Father." Some day, God's kingdom will come in its fullness, but in the meantime, it is our prayer that his kingly rule pervades our lives, takes over our lives, controls us, and then moves out through us to everyone with whom we come into contact. "May your kingdom come."

"Your will be done"

The third imperative is, "Your will be done, may your will be done, on earth as it is in heaven." God's will, his purposes, his desires are always done perfectly in heaven. What the prayer is teaching us is we are to pray like Jesus did Gethsemane; we are to pray, "Not my will, but yours, God, be done." Your will be done, not mine, and may it be done perfectly on earth as it is perfectly done in heaven.

This part of the prayer should come as no surprise to a Christian because being a Christian means we understand that it is no longer all about us. Paul tells the Galatian church, "I have been crucified with Christ. It is no longer I who live, but Christ who lives in me." Jesus says, "you want to be my disciple? Then deny yourself — deny your will and take up your cross. Live every day as someone who has been crucified to himself and this is how you follow me"; this is the whole point of being Christians; it's no longer about us; that's a hard lesson to learn. The temptation keeps coming back, and I say "But it is about me! I don't like the way that you do it, I want..."; that's the way it happens, right? At least it does with me, anyway. I have to constantly remember that it is not about me. Praying the Lord's Prayer is one of those reminders that it is "May your will, my Father, be done and may it be done on earth in me, may it be done on earth around me, and eventually may it be done on earth everywhere! May your will be done on earth, just as it's done in heaven."

Biblical prayer begins with God and it is putting God first. As we pray, "Our Father in heaven," we fade into the background and we become consumed with God and his glory and his praise and his honor; then our lives become no more about all the things that we have done. Prayer teaches us that we move into the adoration and the worship of God, with our praising him for who he is and for what he has done. Prayer begins with worship.

EXPRESS TOTAL DEPENDENCE ON GOD

The second half of the Lord's Prayer takes a little shift because, in the second half, we are taught that prayer is an opportunity for us to express our total dependence on God. I know that it is common in the second half of the Lord's Prayer to say that we get to pray for ourselves; that is not really what is going on. We pray for God's glory at the beginning and then we have this marvelous opportunity to admit our complete and total dependence upon him. So the prayer is still focused on him, even though we are involved.

Self-reliance is not a Christian virtue; self-reliance is a sin. God does not help those who help themselves; that is not in the Bible. God helps those who, in the words of the psalmist, cry out, "You are my Rock. You are my Salvation." "When I am attacked and when times are tough, it is you to Whom I run and it is under your wings that I hide." Self-reliance is a stoical, a worldly, and a sinful attitude. Christ-reliance, complete dependence upon God, is to what God calls us. So total dependence upon God is what the second half of the Lord's Prayer is about.

"Give us this day our daily bread"

In the fourth imperative, we get to admit our total dependence upon him for our physical needs. We pray, "Give us this day our daily bread." God is concerned with the details of our lives. He is concerned with the mundane, the boring, and the normal. He is concerned about our daily bread. What kind of friend would he be if he weren't interested in the details of our lives? I think the point of this fourth imperative, though, is not so much that we pray for food and nothing else. I think the point is that we have the opportunity to admit our dependence upon him for all of our physical needs, which includes things like clothing and shelter.

This is the point that Jesus moves onto later in Matthew 6. In Matthew 6:25 he says, "Therefore I tell you, do not be anxious about your life, what you will eat or what you will drink, nor about your body, what you will put on..." Then he goes on in verse 31, "Therefore do not be anxious, saying, 'What shall we eat?' or 'What shall we drink?' or 'What shall we wear?' For the Gentiles," which in our context is the non-Christian, "seek after all these things, and your heavenly Father knows that you need them all. But seek first the kingdom of God and his righteousness, and all these things will be added," will be simply given, "to you. "Therefore do not be anxious about tomorrow, for tomorrow will be anxious for itself."

Security is an illusion. It is always God upon whom we base our trust for even the most basic things of life. Notice, though, that the promise of Scripture is that God wants to give us our needs, not our "greeds." We are called to pray for daily bread, not yearly bread. At times I find myself praying for yearly bread. "Oh God, do this or that so that I won't have to worry." What I'm really praying for is, "God, I don't want to trust you right now, so I'd rather put enough money into the bank so I don't have to worry about things"; those are our "greeds." The commitment is to trust him. We get the joy of trusting him; in that trust, he provides all that we need day in and day out. "Give us this day our daily bread."

"Forgive us our debts as we forgive our debtors"

The fifth imperative is that we get the chance to express our dependence upon him, not just for our physical needs, but also for our spiritual needs and so we pray, "forgive us our debts as we forgive our debtors." "God, forgive us what we owe you, just as we forgive what other people owe us." Jesus is thinking of sin as a debt — a debt that we owe to God. The payment for that debt, which is forgiveness, comes only from God.

You may be familiar with another translation that interprets the metaphor, "Forgive us our trespasses," our sin, "as we forgive those who trespass against us." Both translations make the same point that we are to come before the throne of grace and ask God to forgive us, just as we have forgiven people who have sinned against us.

Please note the relationship between God's forgiving us and our forgiving others; in fact, this point is so important, and perhaps so difficult to understand and put into practice, that of all the things that Jesus says in the Lord's Prayer, when he gets done, he reviews this point. Verses 14 and 15, "For if you forgive others their trespasses, your heavenly Father will also forgive you; but if you do not forgive others their trespasses, neither will your Father forgive your trespasses."

I hate to be the bearer of bad news, but we are going to be sinned against. We are going to be sinned against perhaps by a friend, perhaps by a co-worker, perhaps by a pastor, or perhaps

by an elder or someone in the church. The temptation — it is
a temptation, but if we yield to it, then it's sin — when we are
sinned against is to cross our arms and, in sinful arrogance
and pride say, "I'm right; they're wrong." "They hurt me and
I'm not going to forgive them until they come crawling to me."
"I'm not going to forgive them until they repent."
"I'm not going to forgive them until they at least admit that
what they did was wrong."

The only person that we truly hurt when we do this is ourselves. If we do not forgive the other person, God will not
forgive us. There is no qualification here that if they repent, if
they admit that they did wrong, if they come crawling to us...;
there is none of that. It simply says, "Forgive or God will not
forgive you." If there is no forgiveness, then all the damage
will come into our relationship with God as the walls come
down and communication is broken.

There are a couple of verses that are very strong on for-
giveness, and I want to emphasize them. Jesus found it nec-
essary to emphasize this point, and that is why we have the
two verses after the Lord's Prayer. (1) Ephesians 4:32 says,
"Be kind, tenderhearted, forgiving one another" when they
have come crawling to you in repentance and sorrow? No!
"Be kind, tenderhearted, forgiving one another, as God in
Christ forgave you." I have been sinned against, just like you.
No one has ever nailed me to the cross before, but I nailed
Jesus to the cross. On the cross, Jesus said, "Father, forgive
Bill Mounce; he doesn't have any idea of what he's doing."
Certainly, if God has forgiven me in Christ, then I can be obe-
dient to him and forgive anyone who has sinned against me;
it is a sign of my true repentance before God. "Be kind, ten-
derhearted, forgiving one another, as God in Christ forgave
you."

(2) The other passage that is actually stronger is in Matthew 18, a few chapters later; it is the parable of the unfor-
giving, unmerciful servant who owed a large sum of dollars
to his master — I mean millions. He plead with his master
to forgive the debt because he couldn't pay it and the master
was a gracious master. He said, "Okay, I forgive your debt."
This unmerciful servant went home and found someone who
owed him a couple hundred dollars, and he refused to forgive

him and had him thrown in jail. His friends didn't like what he had done, so they went to the ungrateful servant's master and told him what happened.

The master called in the unmerciful servant, the one who had been forgiven for a large sum of dollars in debt, and he said to the servant in Matthew 18:32, "'You wicked servant, I forgave you all that debt because you pleaded with me. Should you not have had mercy on your fellow servant as I had mercy on you?' So in anger, the master threw the unmerciful servant in jail." Then in verse 35, Jesus concludes, "So also my heavenly Father will do to every one of you, if you do not forgive your brother from your heart."

"Forgive us our debts, as we forgive our debtors." "Forgive us our trespasses, as we forgive those who trespass against us." It is not an easy thing, but it is a necessary thing.

"And lead us not into temptation, but deliver us from evil."

The sixth and final imperative in the Lord's Prayer is, "And lead us not into temptation, but deliver us from evil." Now, we know from James 1:13 that God doesn't tempt anyone with sin. What Jesus is calling on us to do is to express our dependence upon God, to resist the power of temptation, to resist the power of sin, and to resist the power of evil and the power of the evil one. You and I do not have the capability ourselves to resist evil, especially Satan. "Evil" can also be translated as "Evil One," meaning Satan.

Do you know that verse where Paul says, "We wrestle not against flesh and blood?" I struggle with that verse because I want to put a period there and say, "I don't know about you, Paul, but I wrestle against flesh and blood. I wrestle against my own flesh and blood and I unfortunately end up wrestling against other flesh and blood." But Paul says, "No. In comparison to the realities of life, if you could really knew what's going on, Bill, you don't wrestle against flesh and blood, you wrestle against the spiritual powers — the principalities and the rulers, and you cannot win that battle alone." So we cry out to God in dependence upon him to not allow us into temptation that we cannot resist, but rather to deliver us from evil.

TWO PRACTICAL SUGGESTIONS

That's the Lord's Prayer; that's how he taught his disciples to pray. The Lord's Prayer is the general structure and the general content of how you and I are to pray as well. I want to leave you with two practical suggestions on prayer. There are many things that I could say about prayer. I found it very hard to choose which ones I thought were most important, but let me leave you with two practical suggestions.

1. Speaking with God is a dialogue

The first is about speaking with God; notice the title of this talk. We are not speaking to or at God, but we're speaking *with* God. Healthful communication is always a dialogue. It's always a dialogue. There's always give and take. When Robin and I sit down in the morning, we don't talk *at* each other, we share, going back and forth, we interact, and we mull over things — we speak *with* each other.

One of the things that I have struggled with in prayer is that my mind wanders. Am I the only one? Here we are doing our best, coming before the God who spoke galaxies into existence — he said the words and it happened — standing, sitting or kneeling before the God of galaxies. Then a minute later, we are wondering if we have to mow the lawn today. Then, in comes all the guilt; I just hate that!

About three or four months ago, I was reading from A. W. Tozer and he talked about the same thing. He gave a suggestion that I have put into practice the last couple of months and it has been breathtaking for me. He says, "Don't just start in the morning and pray; it's too hard to keep focused." What he does is start by reading the Bible. (I would encourage you to just read through the Psalms and revolve through them. I always see things I have never seen before.) But start by reading Scripture. As you're reading, listen for the Spirit's promptings. What will happen is that you'll hit a verse and the Spirit will say, "Do you understand that?" Or the Spirit will say, "You need to be encouraged today. I know what is going to happen! You need to be encouraged. Listen to this verse." Or, perhaps the Spirit will say, "You know, that is something you do need to work on." So I would encourage you to read the text but be listening the whole time. As soon as you hear that prompting, stop, reread the verse, and then move into prayer saying, "Okay, Lord, what is it that you want me to see? How do I need to be encouraged or convicted? How do I need to understand or apply this verse?"

So you talk, and then what do you do after you talk? You stay silent — absolutely dead quiet. I don't know about you, but I'm a little hard of hearing physically and spiritually. I know Americans are scared to death of silence. However, when we've heard the promptings of the Spirit of the God of the Universe, and we've asked for help and insight, stop and listen maybe for five minutes. What happens in this process is that we enter into a dialogue with God. It's a bit mysterious, but we enter into this dialogue with God. I find that it is out of the dialogue that I'm able to move into extended times of prayer when I'm not thinking of mowing the backyard. I can go for a long time focused on the God of the Universe — my heavenly Father. That's just a practical suggestion, but it's made more of a difference in my prayer life than anything I've tried to do. Speak *with* God.

Memorize the Lord's Prayer

The second practical suggestion I want to give each of you is to memorize the Lord's Prayer. Do not memorize it just to mindlessly repeat it; it's not some magical incantation; it's not going to get you out of a speeding ticket when you're going to fast. There will be times in our prayer lives where we just can't find the right words. Something is going on, and we're in distress or we're hurt or we realize that we've been caught in sin, or something like that, and the words aren't going to be there. When you find yourself in that situation, say, "My Father, who is in heaven, may your name be holy. May your kingdom come, may your will be done." So I would encourage you to memorize it. Not to mindlessly repeat it, but to have those words when words fail.

The other thing that I would encourage each of you to do is once the Lord's Prayer is memorized, pray the structure of the Lord's Prayer; this is one of my favorite things to do. Once we are aware of the flow of the theology of the Lord's Prayer and understand what those six imperatives are all about, it is possible to go through and start paraphrasing the Lord's Prayer and to start putting in the specifics of our lives.

We're going to do that in just a minute, and I'll show you what I mean. I encourage you to memorize it, to repeat it when you need to, with meaning, and then use your understanding of the theology of the Lord's Prayer and put your own words in there, making it your own prayer. I want to close (together praying the Lord's Prayer) and then I would like to close in prayer myself. Let's pray.

"Our Father in heaven, hallowed be your name. Your kingdom come, your will be done, on earth as it is in heaven. Give us this day our daily bread and forgive us our debts as we also have forgiven our debtors. Lead us not into temptation but deliver us from evil."

6

Learning More about God

When we became Christians, there were certain things that we understood about God. We understood that God existed. We understood that God, the Son, had died for us on the cross for our sin. Hopefully we understood that God, the Holy Spirit, would continue to be present with us to help us and to guide us in our walk. What I would like to do today is perhaps fill out the picture of God in our minds. I want to fill it out by sharing with you three of his attributes — three of his qualities.

My goal in choosing these three is that I want to paint a picture of God's majesty and splendor. I want the picture to call us to a reverence and awe, ultimately calling us to worship him; that was the filter through which I used in choosing the particular three attributes that I did.

Incomprehensibility

However, I need to warn you that God cannot ultimately be known. He cannot be *fully* known, and try as I might with as many big words as I can throw at you, we can never ultimately understand God; it's called his incomprehensibility — he cannot be fully known. God is beyond our ability to understand, and that is why God, through the prophet Isaiah, says, "For as the heavens are higher than the earth, so are my ways higher than your ways and my thoughts higher than your thoughts" (Isaiah 59:9). We cannot fully understand God.

Once we get to heaven, we are still going to keep growing in our knowledge of him. He will still be ultimately incomprehensible. He will continue to be infinite. You and I will continue to be finite; we will continue to be limited in our

knowledge of him. Throughout all of eternity, we will continue to grow to know God, to trust God, to love God, and to
have faith in God; yet we will never achieve a full knowledge
of him, and that is how infinite he is. How great and majestic
and awesome he is.

I have always thought of heaven as a terminus — we go
and all of a sudden we've completely arrived, but that's not
the case. We continue to grow and continue to deepen in our
walk, and there are some things, despite his ultimate incomprehensibility, that God has chosen to reveal to us. I want to
look at three of those attributes:

"OMNISCIENT"

The first is the attribute of God's omniscience. "Omni" is a
form that means "all," so the doctrine of his omniscience is
the doctrine that God knows absolutely everything. In Psalm
139:1-4, the psalmist starts on this note, "O Lord, you have
searched me and known me! You know when I sit down
and when I rise up; you discern my thoughts from afar. You
search out my path and my lying down and are acquainted
with all my ways. Even before a word is on my tongue, behold, O Lord, you know it altogether."

God is omniscient. His omniscience spreads and covers
our thoughts; it spreads to even knowing the words that we
are going to use before we know what we are going to say.
Combined with that is the fact that God not only knows the
present and the past, but God also knows the future. Through
the prophet Isaiah in Isaiah 46:9, he says, "I am God and there
is no other. I am God and there is none like me, declaring the
end from the beginning and from ancient times things not yet
done." The fact that God knows the future is one of the tests
in the prophetical books that he is the true God and all of the
other gods are false gods; from ancient times, only he has de-
clared that he knows what is going to happen.

God knows all things, thoughts, and words — past, present and future. Can you and I really grasp what that means?
Can we really grasp the fact that God knows everything about
everybody? That God knows everything about everything?
He has known everything from the ancient days in the past,

he knows everything about our present, and he has known everything about our future — everything at all times about everybody and everything.

God is as acquainted with the movements of distant galaxies as he is with the number of hairs on our heads and the thoughts before we think them. After eleven marvelous chapters in the book of Romans, after trying to explain the plan of God, Paul finally throws up his hands and he says, "Oh, the depth of the riches and wisdom and knowledge of God! How unsearchable are his judgments and how inscrutable his ways!" (Romans 11:33). After eleven chapters of advanced theology, he says finally, "Who can understand these things about God?"

I don't think it is possible for us to fully understand what it means for God to know everything about everyone and everything, but aren't you glad that he does? Aren't you glad there is nothing that is going to happen to us that God hasn't known about before the creation of time? Aren't you glad that he will never misread us? He will never misunderstand us because he knows us better than we know ourselves. Aren't you glad God is omniscient?

"OMNIPRESENT"

God is not only omniscient, but he is also omnipresent. Omnipresence is the doctrine that God is present everywhere. If you continue to read in Psalm 139:7-12, "Where shall I go from your Spirit? Or where shall I flee from your presence? If I ascend to heaven, you are there! If I make my bed in Sheol," in hell, "You are there! If I take the wings of the morning and dwell in the uttermost parts of the sea, even there your hand shall lead me, and your right hand shall hold me. If I say, 'Surely the darkness shall cover me, and the light about me be night,' even the darkness is not dark to you; for night is bright as the day, for darkness is as light with you."

God is present absolutely everywhere. It's not that God is huge, or it's not even that God is bigger than huge; God simply has no spatial dimension at all. In John 4, when Jesus is talking to the Samaritan woman, he says, "God is Spirit." He didn't say God is a spirit, but what he did say is that he is spirit. "God is Spirit" means he has no spatial dimensions whatsoever, and therefore he exists everywhere in our reality and he exists everywhere in his reality, which is much greater than our reality. God is absolutely everywhere, and so there is no place where God is not present.

When I was younger, I thought of God as being localized — he's everywhere, but he's standing by me and he's sitting by you. I tended to see God as in a specific place, localized here and localized there; that was my view of God without thinking about it. I was in my office one day reading in Acts 17:28, where Paul is talking to the Athenian philosophers. Paul is trying to emphasize that God is not an idol, and so he says, "In him," in God, "we live and move and have our being." The verse stopped me and I started mulling it over. "In him, we live and move and have our being"; that's kind of a mystical thought. What does that mean? It was one of those surreal moments in my life when the air from the fan hit me and reminded me of the passage in John 4. Jesus makes the comparison of wind blowing wherever it wants to and you can hear its sound — it's a pun in John because the same words can be translated as "Spirit speaks and you hear his voice." A comparison is going on between wind and spirit, and it hit me that just as you and I exist in wind and in air — it's everywhere around us and we all exist in it — so also you and I exist in God. We live and we move and have our being in God.

We are not pantheists; we do not believe that the wind is God. However, we believe that God created all things and yet is separate from all creation. Yet Paul says to pagan philosophers, "In God we live and we move and we have our being." It was a mind-bending experience for me as I started to realize that God isn't localized, standing next to me or sitting next to you, but he's absolutely everywhere. Just as you and I live in air, and just as the galaxies exist in space, all things — you, me, and the millions of stars and galaxies — exist in God; we live and move in him; we have our being in him. That's the omnipresence of God.

You can add to that, too! It's not like God is thinly spread throughout all creation. Do you ever think that way? "If he's everywhere, there's only a little piece of him here and a little piece there." God is present in his fullness in every place in creation; that's why we have his undivided attention when we pray to God. While he is everywhere, he is in every specific locale in his fullness and in his completeness.

Are you able to grasp that? I can't! But aren't you glad that God is omnipresent. Aren't you glad that, even when we want to, there is no place that we can go and hide from him? He is there, wherever we go. In the language of the Psalms, even if we go someplace and call for the rocks to fall on us, he is there. We cannot run from him. Aren't you glad there is no place where God is not present to help, to encourage, to love, and to instruct us? Even in our thoughts, God is fully present. God is an omnipresent God; he is everywhere.

"OMNIPOTENT"

Not only is God omnipresent, but he is also omnipotent. He is our omni-potentate. He is all powerful. The word that we tend to use for this, along with "omnipotence," is "sovereign." God is a sovereign God, which means that God exercises his sovereign rule, or his kingly rule, over his creation. He is sovereign; he is omnipotent.

If we continue in Psalm 139:13-16, the psalmist says this precisely. "For you formed my inward parts; you knitted me together in my mother's womb. I praise you, for I am fearfully and wonderfully made. Wonderful are your works; my soul knows it very well. My frame was not hidden from you, when I was being made in secret, intricately woven in the depths of the earth" — the psalmist's metaphor for his mother's womb. "Your eyes saw my unformed substance; in your book were written," every one of them, "the days that were formed for me, when as yet there was none of them." In praising God, the psalmist points out that, "You formed my life. You are a powerful God. You wrote out the days of my life, even before I existed. You are a powerful God." Elsewhere in the Psalms he writes, "Our God is in the heavens; he does all that he pleases." The biblical definition for omnipotence is that God can do anything he wants to do; there are no limits on the exercise of his will.

Once again, I would suggest that this is an attribute of God that we simply cannot fully grasp, but aren't you glad that God is omnipotent? That he is sovereign over his creation? Aren't you glad that we can know with absolute assuredness that the book of Revelation is true? God is so powerful that we can be absolutely confident that at the end of time, God wins and Satan loses. You see, that is the omnipotence of God, that he can make it happen. Aren't you glad that God is omnipotent?

So when we read that nothing can separate us from the love of God in Christ Jesus, we know that the strongest force in reality has guaranteed that nothing can separate you and me from the love of God in Christ Jesus — nothing. Even in the midst of pain, we are able to entrust our souls to an all-powerful God. Even when things are as bad as they can get, God is an omnipotent God, and we know that he can carry us through; this is the point Peter is making in 1 Peter 4:19, "Therefore let those who suffer according to God's will entrust their souls to a faithful Creator while doing good." Even when you and I are suffering and being persecuted for our faith because we are Christians, God is still an all-powerful God; entrusting ourselves to him is still the best thing to do. God is omniscient, omnipresent, and omnipotent. This is our God; this is our heavenly Father into whose arms we leapt when we became children of God; this is our heavenly Father in whose arms we live.

MY RESPONSE: WORSHIP

The question then becomes: How are you and I going to respond? This question isn't an academic inquiry in Theology 401! How are you are I going to respond? There is only one way to respond and that is in worship. The only appropriate response when we are faced with the activities and attributes of God is to worship. Because worship is so important, we need to have a clear understanding of it worship is.

"Worth-ship"

For those of you who are new Christians, you may not understand right now that the church is caught up in the throws of the worship wars, trying to figure out what worship is.

I'll tell you right up front that singing isn't worship. Are you aware of that? Singing isn't worship. A song can become an instrument of worship, but coming in and singing for a half hour isn't necessarily worship.

What then is worship? What is its definition? The English comes from the forms "worth" and "ship." The word worship was formed to mean attributing worth. The Greek and the Hebrew words that lie behind the English translation of worship carry the ideas of bowing down and serving. One definition I've heard of worship is, "bowing all that we are before all that God is." It's a great definition of worship.

Response to God's revelation

Another definition that I want to talk about is that worship is "our faithful response to God's gracious revelation." Worship is an appropriate response when God reveals his attributes and his activities to us, which means that worship begins with hearing.

Worship begins with hearing what God is like — his attributes. Worship begins with hearing about the activities of God, who he is, and what he is doing. That is why one of the things that we work at so hard in a church is to emphasize the clarity of the revelation. Our drive for making sure the revelation of God is clear has affected many things we do here on Sunday morning; it affects the amount of money we've spent on the speakers, the kind of soundboard we bought, and the shape of the room. Our belief that the clarity of the revelation of God's attributes and activity pervade so much of what we do that it affects how I preach. Above all else, I am not here to entertain you. I am here to express, with clarity, the activities and attributes of God, so that you can hear it. A desire for clarity in the revelation of God affects our reading of God's Word, how we pray, and how we sing. The lyrics in our songs must be correct. The volume of the melody cannot overpower the strength of the lyrics. We work for clarity all the time because worship involves the clear revelation of the attributes and the activities of God, and that pervades almost everything we do.

Worship isn't just hearing. Worship is also responding appropriately. As one person has said, "Worship is not a spectator sport; worship is not sitting in the stands; we must respond." We must respond to the revelation of God. If the attributes and the activities of God are laid out before us and there's no response, there's no worship; we must respond.

Isaiah 6

Worship isn't entertainment either. Worship is not about me, nor is it about how I feel. Worship is the declaration with clarity of the activity and the attributes of God, and then it is our appropriate response. If you want to be entertained, my suggestion is to stay home and read a book; that's not what this is about.

There are a lot of places where we could go in Scripture to talk about this, but the most powerful passage is the passage in Isaiah 6, where you can see what real biblical worship is. Here we see three cycles of worship.

Cycle 1

Starting at verse 1, "In the year that King Uzziah died I saw the Lord," he had a vision or he was taken to heaven; one of the two, "sitting upon a throne, high and lifted up; and the train of his robe filled the temple. Above him stood the seraphim," special angelic creatures. "Each had six wings: with two he covered his face, and with two he covered his feet, and with two he flew. And one called to another and said: 'Holy, holy, holy is the Lord of hosts; the whole earth is full of his glory!' And the foundations of the thresholds shook at the voice of him who called, and the house was filled with smoke."

The seraphim know how to worship. They understand the revelation of God as they fly before him for all eternity, as far as we know. God has given them six wings so that their response will be appropriate to the revelation. With two wings, each of them covers their own eyes. With two wings, each covers their own feet. With two wings they can fly so they can stand there in the constant anthem of "Holy, holy, holy is the Lord God Almighty." The seraphim are responding to the revelation of God appropriately; they are worshiping him.

This is the revelation that Isaiah gets — what Isaiah sees and experiences. So the question is, how is Isaiah going to respond to the revelation? "And I said: 'Woe is me! For I am lost; for I am a man of unclean lips, and I dwell in the midst of a people of unclean lips; for my eyes have seen the King, the Lord of hosts!'" (Isaiah 6:5). That is worship! Isaiah was given a vision of heaven; he was shown God, the seraphim, and the ongoing worship that is happening all the time in heaven while we're down here. He responds appropriately with acknowledging his sin and his unworthiness to be in the presence of God. "I want to see you, Lord, I want to see you high and lifted up"; we sing this song a lot here, and every time we sing it, I think, "Do you all really know what you're saying?" "Do you really understand what you're asking?" Because if you and I say, "We want to see you, Lord," and we do see him, we are not going to be standing with smiles on our faces with our hands outstretched! We're going to be flat on our faces groveling before him, because we are going to see, more clearly than any other time in our lives, that we are sinners worthy of nothing but hell.

So the next time you and I sing that song, let's think through what we are really asking, because when Isaiah saw the Lord "high and lifted up," he fell flat on his face, because it was the only appropriate thing to do. When we see God's holiness, we understand our sin, and that is worship.

Cycle 2

Confession is a large part of worship. What is interesting in the Isaiah story is it appears that because Isaiah responded properly, God chooses to reveal more; so the story continues. "Then one of the seraphim flew to me, having in his hand a burning coal that he had taken with tongs from the altar. And he touched my mouth and said: 'Behold, this has touched your lips; your guilt is taken away, and your sin atoned for'" (Isaiah 6:6-7).

God is revealing to Isaiah that he is a God of mercy and the source of forgiveness; he is willing to forgive. Isaiah responded appropriately in confession and worship, so God reveals more saying, "I'm a God of mercy." He didn't say, "you know, Isaiah, you're a pretty good guy; I've got some use for you. I'll forgive you so you can go do my work; you've earned it." No! God is a God of mercy, who simply sends the seraphim with coal to touch his lips and say, "you are forgiven."

While it is not stated specifically, it certainly is implicit that Isaiah responded properly, therefore, he received God's free, merciful gift of forgiveness. When you read this story you might say, "Yes, but so would anyone else." But how many times have you received the free offer of God's mercy and grace to a sinner, and you've said, "No, I don't want it"?

Cycle 3

Isaiah responded in worship; he allowed the seraphim to touch his lips. Because he responded properly in worship, there is more revelation: "And I heard the voice of the Lord saying, "Whom shall I send, and who will go for us?" God is revealing that he has a will, that he has work to be done, he has revelation he needs to transmit.

How else would Isaiah respond to this revelation other than how he did, saying, "here am I, send me." Notice he didn't say, "God, tell me what you want me to do first." "How much is this going to cost me?" "Am I going to have to leave my home?" "Will I be happy?" "Will I feel good about myself?" Isaiah just says, "here am I, send me," which is the only appropriate response in worship to the revelation that God has a will — he has a desire for your life and for mine. This should be the normative response for all believers.

I understand that for those of you who are new in your faith, this concept might be a bit overwhelming, but you need to know that this is what's coming; this is what God has asked of us. True worshipers are those who understand God's will; they understand God's mercy and holiness. When we look in the face of those truths about God, we worship when we hear it, and we worship when we respond appropriately by confessing our sin, receiving the free gift of forgiveness and saying, "Here am I; send me."

My prayer for this church and each one of you is that this becomes the normative response in worship for you. I pray that when you worship you say with abandon, "here I am, whatever! I believe you are all good; I believe you are all wise. I believe you have my best interests, but ultimately you have your best interests at heart. I am a tool of yours. I can't wait to get going." Do you know what would happen in this city

if we did that? Can you imagine what a church unleashed
would look like in this town if all of us were to respond as we
should respond, as Isaiah responded?

NEVER LET GOD BECOME SMALL

The challenge of Isaiah 6, the challenge of theology, the challenge of knowing the attributes and activity of God, is first
and foremost to never let God become small. Never let God
become a little localized deity. Never think that we know
more than he knows or think that we can hide from him. Never think that he isn't powerful enough to help us in our puny
little problems; we have to keep these things in perspective.
When we look at the things going on in our lives and realize
that the God to whom we pray is omniscient and omnipotent
and omnipresent, and he loves us, how can we not respond in
worship? Why do we worry? Why do we get anxious? Why
do we say, "God helps those who help themselves?" Why do
we do that? The answer is sin — if you were looking for an
answer!

As you and I grow in our Christian walk, may our understanding of God grow with us. May we understand that the
God whom we serve, the God who loves us, is without limit
in everything.

He is without limit in terms of his wisdom. He is omniscient; he knows us better than we know ourselves, and he
still loves us.

God is without limitation in his presence. God is omnipresent; he has no spatial dimensions. You and I, our community, and the galaxies in the universe all exist in him; he
is bigger than that because all of his reality is in him as well.

God is without limitation of power; he is our omni-potentate, and mighty to save.

May we never just sit and not respond to that. May our
responses always be appropriate for what God has revealed
to us, which means we must be quick to acknowledge his holiness and our sin, and quick to receive his mercy and his
grace. We need to be quick to do his will, even if we don't
know what it is. We need to raise our hands and say, "Here
am I Lord. I'm your child. Send me."

When we get to heaven, we will see him clearly; not dimly as in a mirror, but face to face. You and I, who are children of God, get to spend all of eternity constantly growing in our knowledge of him and our love for him, and we will continue to worship him more and more each day forever and ever and ever. That's our God. Aren't you glad you're his child?

7

Learning More about Who Jesus Is

WHO IS JESUS?

This was the central question of the early church; it was the central question of Paul's preaching. Paul tells the Corinthians, "I decided to know nothing among you except Jesus Christ and him crucified." The question of who is Jesus is the preoccupation of the first four books of the New Testament, as the gospels tell us about the life and the death and the resurrection of Jesus Christ. In fact, our very name as "Christians" shows that we are not primarily about doctrine, fellowship, or religion, but we are first and foremost preoccupied with Jesus Christ and who he is.

Who is Jesus is the central question of all reality and it is paramount that all Christians have a clear answer to this question. There are a lot of common answers to this question. If we were to go down and stand on the street and ask people, "Who do you think Jesus is?" We would get a wide range of answers. We would certainly hear someone say that he was a good man, he was a teacher, he was a prophet, or the founder of a religion. We may get someone that says that he was demon-possessed; that's what some people of Jesus' day thought. Perhaps we might run across someone who said, "Oh, he's a lesser god — a created being and Satan's brother." If you asked Albert Schweitzer, supposedly the greatest Christian of the last century, he would say that Jesus Christ died a deluded, raving fanatic on the cross. If we were to ask others who Jesus was, we might hear something like, "Don't know; don't care."

There is a wide range of answers to the question of who is

Jesus, and yet everything in life and in death hinges on this question. This is one of those questions where there is a right answer and there are wrong answers. As we stand before the Judgment Seat of God, there will only be one right answer to the question of who Jesus is.

ACTS 2

The book of Acts tells the story of the early church. In chapter 2, we read Peter's first sermon, which was delivered to answer this question of who is Jesus. In Acts 2:22-24, Peter says, "men of Israel, hear these words: Jesus of Nazareth, a man attested to you by God with mighty works and wonders and signs that God did through him in your midst, as you yourselves know this Jesus, delivered up according to the definite plan and foreknowledge of God, you crucified" — he must have had some impact saying it that way — "and killed by the hands of lawless men. But God raised him up, loosing the pangs of death, because it was not possible for him to be held by it."

Then Peter goes into a discussion of a prophecy by King David a thousand years previous, a prophecy about Jesus. Then in verse 32 he says, "'This Jesus God raised up, and of that we all are witnesses.' And Jesus, 'Being therefore exalted at the right hand of God, and,' you and I, 'having received from the Father the promise of the Holy Spirit, he has poured out this that you yourselves are seeing and hearing,' the gift of the Holy Spirit.' He continues in verse 36, 'Let all the house of Israel therefore know for certain that God has made him both Lord and Christ, this Jesus whom you crucified.' Now when they heard this they were cut to the heart, and said to Peter and the rest of the apostles, 'Brothers, what shall we do?' And Peter said to them, 'Repent and be baptized every one of you in the name of Jesus Christ for the forgiveness of your sins, and you will receive the gift of the Holy Spirit.'" Peter continued to preach for a while and three thousand people became Christians. So his preaching is all about this question, "Who is Jesus?"

In verse 38, when he calls them to repent, certainly part of the repentance is repenting from sin, but first and foremost,

Peter was calling them to repent of their misunderstanding of who Jesus is; that is what the whole sermon was about: "Who is Jesus?" The repentance is a call that they turn aside from what they had thought about Jesus and turn to Peter's definition, Peter's understanding, of who Jesus is.

REAL HUMAN BEING

Who is Jesus? Notice that Peter starts with the name, Jesus of Nazareth. Part of the Gospel message is certainly that Jesus was a real human being. He was born to Mary and Joseph, peasants without rank, fame, or fortune. He grew up in a small town called Nazareth, an insignificant wide spot in the road in an insignificant country — as far as the world was concerned. When Jesus was 30, he gathered twelve men around him as his followers and for three-and-one-half years he preached. He got tired; he ate; he slept. He never got married, contrary to a popular lie. He never owned a house. He never traveled far from home. Yet he was seen as a religious rebel; he was seen as a threat to the religious establishment. After three-and-one-half years, he was deserted by his friends and killed by his own countrymen. Jesus of Nazareth was a very real human being who went through a lot of same kinds of experiences that you and I do.

JESUS IS LORD

Peter makes it clear that he is not just Jesus of Nazareth. As Peter preaches, we realize that this Jesus is much more than a mere human being. In verse 36, Peter makes the point that by means of the resurrection, God has made it clear that this Jesus is also Lord. What does Lord mean? In the Greek, it is *kyrios*; you may have heard it before. *Kyrios* is a difficult word to translate because it has a wide range of meanings. *Kyrios* can mean sir, a term of polite address. *Kyrios* can mean master; when a servant would talk to his master, the servant would most likely call his master *kyrios*.

There's another use of *kyrios* that is more significant here. In the Greek translation of the Old Testament, the Greek word *kyrios* was used to translate the most holy name of God in the entire Old Testament, the name of "Yahweh," "Jehovah," two different ways of pronouncing the same name.

Kyrios is the name that Moses gets in the story of the burning bush in Exodus 3, a story in the Old Testament. Moses walks by a bush that is burning and it's not burning up, so he walks over to see it. God speaks out of the burning bush, and in the course of the discussion Moses says, "What's your name?" God replies out of the burning bush, "I AM who I AM"; it's that name I AM that comes into English as Yahweh or Jehovah; it's that name that was translated with *kyrios* in the Greek Old Testament.

JESUS IS THE SON OF GOD

What Peter is preaching in Acts 2 is that Jesus is God, Jesus is the great I AM of the burning bush in Exodus 3. The theme of Jesus' being God runs all the way through the New Testament.

Beginning at Jesus' birth, when we read the birth narratives in the gospel of Matthew, you can see Matthew reminding us that about 700 years before the time of Christ, Isaiah made a prophecy that a virgin would conceive and have a child. 700 years later, the Virgin Mary did conceive and did have a child. When the angel came to tell Mary that this was going to happen, she was understandably a little confused as to what was going on.

In Luke 1:35, the angel explains how this is going to happen: "And the angel answered her, 'The Holy Spirit will come upon you, and the power of the Most High will overshadow you; therefore the child to be born will be called holy — the Son of God.'" So even at the announcement of Jesus' birth, the phrase, Son of God, is being used to describe him.

The phrase, Son of God, is used all the way through the New Testament to continue to describe Jesus. For example, why did John write the fourth gospel? What was the purpose to his writing? He tells us at the very end in chapter 20. John says, "these things are written so that you may believe that Jesus is the Christ, the Son of God."

Also, the title of the gospel of Mark, in 1:1, is "The beginning of the gospel of Jesus Christ, the Son of God"; that verse functions as Mark's title for the gospel. Mark is writing to let us know that Jesus was not just a man, he was not just a human being, but he was, in fact, the Son of God. What is interesting as we read through Mark, the title "Son of God" only occurs two other times: In chapter 5, the demons say, "We know who you are, you are the Holy Son of God." Then most importantly, after his death a centurion says, "This surely is the Son of God." We might ask, "Mark, if your purpose in writing is to prove that Jesus is the Son of God, shouldn't you say it a little more often?" Mark would say, "Oh Bill, not everything has to be taught in explicit theological statements. If you want that, go to the gospel of John; that's what he is about."

What Mark does is he teaches Christ's divinity implicitly in the stories he tells. When we read the stories in Mark of what Jesus did and what he taught, we realize that this is the Son of God. We don't have to get very far into Mark to realize that Jesus has power over sickness, he has power over demons, and he has power over the natural world; he can even calm the troubled Sea of Galilee. Jesus has power over death; he can raise Jarius' daughter from the dead. Jesus has authority to forgive sin — something that belongs to God and to God alone. As we read the initial chapters in Mark, we will realize quickly that we are reading about someone who is no mere person, but that he must be much more than a person in order to do what he does — he must be the Son of God.

I need to mention that when you and I, as English speakers, hear the phrase, Son of God, it's really easy to misunderstand what that phrase means. The Bible can use "son" with the way that Tyler and Hayden are my sons, but the Bible can also use the phrase "son" in a significantly different meaning, and it's easy to misunderstand it. For example, the Mormons have misunderstood this phrase. For a Mormon, Jesus is a created lesser being — Satan's brother; that is not what the phrase means in the Bible. We have got to understand that Jesus lived in a tremendously monotheistic culture; there was one God, and one only God, and everything fit under the rubric; they had not figured out the Trinity yet.

When Jesus starts using language such as, "I am the Son," or "I am the Son of God," or "God is my Father," when Jesus used that kind of familial language, the Jews of his day understood exactly what he was saying. They understood that he was claiming to be equal with God.

The best passage to see this is in John 5. All that Jesus said in verse 17 was, "My Father is working until now, and I am working." Jesus had healed someone on the Sabbath, which was a big no-no in Jewish ritual. In verse 18 we read, "This was why the Jews were seeking all the more to kill him, because not only was he breaking the Sabbath," he wasn't following their little rules, "but he was even calling God his own Father, making himself equal with God." So in Jesus' original context, when he talks about himself being the Son and God being his Father, and when the Bible talks about Jesus being the Son of God, it's not some lesser created being. Jesus is claiming to be God himself.

JESUS IS GOD

The Bible also explicitly calls Jesus God. The Bible doesn't always use the phrase "Son of God"; sometimes it just calls him God. John 1:1, "In the beginning was the Word and the Word was with God and the Word was God." As you read on in John 1, we realize that the Word is a philosophical concept that is being applied to Jesus, who is God. By the way, when the Jehovah Witnesses come and say there's no "the" in front of "was God," and they say God is with a small "g," just ask them to repeat the Greek alphabet — they probably don't know Greek. The Bible does not say Jesus was a god, it says Jesus was God, capital "G." If they want to argue, I've got a great Greek grammar book they can look at written by Dan Wallace and he will show them why. "In the beginning was the Word and the Word was with God and the Word was God"; capital "G," if you know Greek.

Just eighteen verses later John says, "No one has ever seen God; the only God, who is at the Father's side, he has made him known." The "only God" is not God the Father because the "only God" is at the Father's side. So the "only God" is Jesus, who is the Only God.

Jesus himself claimed to be God. He was arguing with the Jews once again, and in John 8, he says, "before Abraham was," before Abraham even existed, "I am." I know if we're reading in English and if we're not familiar with the Old Testament, we would simply say, "I am ... what?" However, the Jews understood exactly what he was saying, because they tried to kill him for it; that was the penalty for blasphemy. Jesus said, "Before Abraham was 'I am.'" "I am the great I AM." "I am Yahweh." "I am the Jehovah of the burning bush who said, 'I am *Kyrios*. I am God."

Later on Jesus says in John 10:30, "I and the Father are one."

Thomas was one of Jesus' disciples, a Jew, and was intensely monotheistic. Yet when Thomas sees the risen Lord, his response was "My Lord and my God."

Paul, talking to his friend Titus, refers to "our great God and Savior, Jesus Christ."

Peter talks about the righteousness of our "God and Savior, Jesus Christ."

There are many more verses and many more arguments that I could bring, but it is clear that the Bible claims that Jesus claimed, that his disciples claimed, and that his apostles claimed, that Jesus was, in fact, God.

ALLOWING FOR THE TRINITY

One of the interesting things in this whole mix is that the biblical writers are having to allow for the Trinity; remember our discussion on that? We are monotheists: "hear O Israel, the Lord our God, the Lord is one." We believe in one God. Yet we believe in the Trinity — a Godhead: God the Father, God the Son, God the Holy Spirit. All three are fully God and yet all three together are God; it's a mystery. We can't expect to understand fully the things of God. So we can see in the way in which the words are used in the New Testament, the writers are trying to make allowance for the fact that there is a Trinity.

For example, Jesus doesn't say, "I and the Father are exactly the same thing." They are not. There's God the Father, God the Son, and there's God the Holy Spirit; and yet, there is one God. The language has to deal with the reality of the Trinity, and yet these are all explicit claims that Jesus is God.

With that as background, we can come back to the use of

the word Lord in Acts 2, and we can see what Peter's preaching. Peter is preaching that by means of Jesus' resurrection, God has made it explicitly clear that Jesus is Lord, he is *Kyrios*, he is Yahweh, he is the great I AM, he is the Son of God, and he is God. That's the amplified version of Acts 2:36.

INCARNATION

Fully human

What we're dealing with here is the doctrine of the "Incarnation" of Jesus. The doctrine of the incarnation is that God became incarnate; that God became flesh. Stated another way: the incarnation is the doctrine that Jesus was fully God and fully human. Both sides to that equation are important because on one hand, Jesus did not just appear to be a human being, but Jesus was fully human. In John 1:14, he says, "And the Word," Jesus, "became flesh and dwelt among us." John uses the most basic word that he can in Greek to describe this stuff that is hanging off our bones; Jesus became flesh. There's no concept in the Bible that says Jesus was human on the outside and God on the inside. Jesus was every bit as human as we are human.

Yet Scripture does point out that while he is fully human, he nevertheless lived without sin. In the book of Hebrews, chapter 4, the author is talking about the fact that Jesus is our high priest. Jesus stands between God the Father and us, interceding for us. In Hebrews 4 starting in verse 15, it says, "For we do not have a high priest who is unable to sympathize with our weaknesses, but one who in every respect has been tempted as we are, yet without sin."

That's one of the beauties of the doctrine of the incarnation.

When we pray to God, we understand that our Lord and Savior, Jesus Christ, is always before the throne interceding for us. We know that Jesus can sympathize with every thing that is happening to us, because he was fully human and he went through the same kinds of trials that you and I did, and yet he did so without sin. Later on in Hebrews chapter 7, he's talking again about Jesus' being a high priest, and he uses words like holy and innocent and unstained and separated from sinners. Jesus didn't just appear to be human, he was fully human, and yet he was fully human without sin.

Fully God

The other side of the incarnation equation is just as true, which is while Jesus was fully human, he also was fully God. How many times have you heard someone say, "Oh, I just believe Jesus was a good man"? Have we not heard that more times than we care to hear? The fact of the matter is that good people don't say the things that Jesus said. If Jesus were only human and nothing else, we can't call him a good person. Good people don't go around saying things like, "I am the vine and you are the branches. Unless you abide in me and I in you, you can't bear any fruit."

I feel so bad for Jesus' brothers and sisters! "Mom, he's doing it again: he's telling everyone he's the vine." We've got to have patience with his brothers and sisters; talk about having a perfect big brother! Good people don't go around saying things like "I and the Father are one." We lock them up when they do that.

It's sad how many of our institutions are full of people who think they are Jesus, who think they are Christ, and who think they are God. People in control of their mental facilities, and if they're good people, don't say the kinds of things that Jesus said. Anyone who says, "I believe that Jesus was a good man," simply hasn't read the Bible; you can't read the Bible and come away with that understanding.

As has often been said, either Jesus is a liar of pathological proportions, or he's a lunatic, mentally unstable, or he is exactly who he said he is — he is God; there is no fourth option.

IMPORTANCE OF THE INCARNATION

Jesus is fully God and fully human; that's the doctrine of the incarnation. The questions are: Is it important to believe this? Is it important to understand it? The answer, obviously, is yes. The incarnation, if nothing else, is the greatest miracle that ever happened; it's the miracle of God becoming human. I think there are, at least, two good reasons why we need to be focused on the incarnation and to believe and understand it:

1. Important to our salvation

The first reason has to do with our salvation. The only way that salvation could be a possibility for you and for me is for Jesus to have been the God-man, which is a term that theologians like to use. If Jesus were not the God-man, he could not have provided salvation, and you and I would still be dead in our trespasses and in our sin.

On the one hand, the Bible says that he had to be fully human if he was going to be the sacrifice for human sin; there is something in the justice of God that requires human death for human sin. The book of Hebrews expounds on this in 2:17 where it says that Jesus, "had to be made like his brothers in every respect, so that he," Jesus, "might become a merciful and faithful high priest in the service of God." If he were not human, he couldn't be our high priest, "to make propitiation," a sacrifice, "for the sins of the people." Jesus had to be like you and me if he was going to be the sacrifice for our sin. I don't know why that's the case, but it has to do with the heart of God and his justice. Jesus had to be fully human; and if Jesus were not fully human; then there would be no sacrifice, which means you and I would still be in our sin on our way to hell. Are we not glad that Jesus was fully human?

Also, in order for salvation to be a reality, Jesus had to be fully God.

No human being could have carried the weight of all the world's sin (past, present, and future) for those hours he hung on the cross; none of us are capable of bearing that kind of weight.

Jesus had to be fully God because no human being could live a perfect life. If Jesus had not lived a perfect life, there would be no perfect death that could be given sacrificially for you and me.

No human being's death could be applied to our sin. If somehow we were enabled to live a perfect life, why would we think that our death could pay the penalty for someone else's sin, much less the whole world's sin?

Jesus had to be fully God in order for these things to happen because ultimately, salvation belongs to our God; therefore, Jesus had to be God. The refrain comes from Psalm 3:8, and it's elaborated in Revelation 7:10, that "salvation belongs to our God."

Our salvation is absolutely dependent upon the incarnation, the full humanity of Christ, so that his death would be a human death, and the full divinity of Christ, so that his death could be applied to you and to me. Without the incarnation, we're all dead and on our way to hell.

Ramifications

There are some amazing ramifications that come out of this truth. Let me just mention two in passing:

1. Christianity is exclusive

If you and I can come to grips with the incarnation and what it means, then at a very deep level we will understand why Christianity is so exclusive. Throughout history, Christians have been accused of being prideful and arrogant because they think that they are the only way to God, that they're better than the Hindus, and that they're better than the Muslims.

Let us not forget the fact that it was Jesus who said, "I am the way, and the truth, and the life. No one comes to the Father but by me." The reason for that is that there has never been another God-man. There has never been a God-man who is the single mediator between God and humanity (I Timothy 2:5). There was no other time in which God became a human sacrifice for human sin applied to all people. Yes, we are incredibly exclusive; all roads do not lead to God; all but one road leads straight to hell. It's not because we're prideful and arrogant people, it's because there's only one God-man, Jesus Christ, and there is no other way to God.

2. Evangelism must be radically Christ-centered

The other ramification is that this doctrine of incarnation must have an impact on our evangelism. It means, among other things, that there is no other name given among human beings whereby we must be saved. If people do not hear the good news of Jesus Christ, they will die in their sin and spend an eternity in hell; there is no other way to come into the presence of the Father. We must take that seriously, all the way from our offerings and our church budget to what we say to our neighbors and how we talk to our friends; there is no other way to get to heaven other than through Jesus Christ, the one God-man.

It also means that our evangelism must be radically God-centered, must be radically Christ-centered. People love to pull us off track; don't they?

"What do you think of Jesus?" "I don't know. I don't know if I can believe in a religion where God sends people to hell." "That's an interesting question, but what about Jesus." "Oh, I'm not sure I can believe in a God who, supposedly, is all good and all powerful but let's evil exist."

"That's a good questions, but what about Jesus." "Oh, I can't believe in a God. The Bible is full of mistakes." "Interesting question, you can point them out to me later. What about Jesus?"

Our evangelism, our talking with neighbors and friends and co-workers, has to be radically centered on the person of Jesus Christ because that's the question that matters. It's the answer to that question that will get people in heaven and paradise and glory forever or will send them to hell forever.

Who is Jesus? He is the incarnate God. He is God. He is human. Because he is the only God-man, he's the only avenue to God or access to living with him forever in heaven.

The doctrine of the incarnation is anything but academic. It pervades and controls our very lives, our salvation, and the offer of salvation to other people. The doctrine of incarnation is important when it comes to salvation.

2. You must believe in the incarnation to be a Christian

The second reason why the doctrine of incarnation is so important is because if you don't believe it, you're not a Christian. Let's talk about the minimum amount that we need to share in the gospel presentation, so that if someone responds to it, he or she becomes a Christian.

I'll ask people, "What is the minimum it takes to get into heaven?" They often say, "I don't like that question." No? You're at the bus stop, and you've got two minutes. You can see the bus coming and you've got this person who's asked you about Jesus, and the clock starts ticking. (It happened to me once — I didn't have an answer.) We see the bus coming, and all of a sudden it becomes a very relevant question, doesn't it? While some of us are sitting here saying, "That's not a good question! We shouldn't be asking that question," the minutes are ticking and the bus is getting closer.

To be a Christian, we must believe in the incarnation. We must believe in the full humanity of Christ. In 1 John 4, John is talking about the false teaching that was going on; the false teachers denied the humanity of Christ. They were struggling with the idea of God's dying, but John says in 1 John 4:2, "By this you know the Spirit of God," by this you know if someone is a Christian, "every spirit," or every person, "that confesses that Jesus Christ has come in the flesh is from God, and every spirit that does not confess Jesus is not from God; this is the spirit of the antichrist." So John says that one of the minimal required beliefs in order to be a follower of God is to believe that Jesus is fully human.

If we are Christians, we also must believe in the full divinity of Christ, so we're back to the word "Lord." Paul is talking to the Roman church, Romans 10: 9: "If you confess with your mouth that Jesus is *Kyrios*, and believe in your heart that God raised him from the dead, you will be saved." In Romans 10:9, we have this helpful mixing of both halves of the incarnation: we have to believe that God raised him from the dead; that's a physical resurrection of a real human being, and yet we also must confess that Jesus is *Kyrios*; that he is Yahweh. So the doctrine of the incarnation is extremely important.

CENTRAL QUESTION OF LIFE

The central question of life is who Jesus is; it should pervade everything that we do. If our understanding of who Jesus is, is different from Peter's, if our understanding of who Jesus is, is different from what I've explained, then in the words of Peter, we are called to repent. We are called to repent of our false understanding of who Jesus is. We know once we do that, then repentance from sin and all the other things will follow. If we do believe in the incarnation — Jesus is fully God and fully man — then the challenge of the incarnation is to allow that truth to pervade everything that we do. Because there's only one God-man, there is only one way to God, and there is only one means to salvation — all the other roads of religions, sincerity, and religious activity lead to the gates of hell. Only the road through the God-man goes to heaven; may that be our challenge in the doctrine of the incarnation.

8

Learning More about What Jesus Did

There is a character in the New Testament called John the Baptist, and he was quite a character. Part of his job was to prepare the way for Jesus' coming. When he did see Jesus coming, he cried out, "Behold, the Lamb of God who takes away the sin of the world" (John 1:29). This is an important verse if we are going to understand what Jesus did on the cross.

The technical term for what Jesus did on the cross is "Atonement," which is what actually happened when the Lamb of God died on the cross and took away the sin of the world.

JESUS IS THE LAMB OF GOD

When John calls Jesus a lamb, he's not making reference to some cute farm animal, but he's making reference to the fact that Jesus is the sacrificial lamb; Jesus was going to be a lamb who would be sacrificed. There is no better place to go to understand what that means than in the book of Leviticus in the Old Testament. Leviticus is all about explaining the holiness of God, the sinfulness of all human beings, and specifically how God goes about forgiving sin.

Turn in your Bibles, please, to the book of Leviticus in chapter 1. The scenario is that someone has sinned, and in order to be forgiven of his sin, he's going to make a sacrifice. The question is, how do we make a sacrifice. Here is one of the many sets of instructions on how we do that. In Leviticus 1:10 it says, "If his gift," the sinner's, "for a burnt offering is from the flock, from the sheep or goats, he shall bring a male without blemish," not defective, the best you have, "and he," the sinner who is bringing the animal, not the priest, "shall kill it on the north side of the altar before the Lord, and Aaron's sons the priests shall throw its blood against the sides of the altar. And he," the sinner, "shall cut it into pieces, with its head and its fat, and the priest shall arrange them on the wood that is on the fire on the altar, but the entrails," the guts, "and the legs he shall wash with water. And the priest shall offer all of it and burn it on the altar; it is a burnt offering, a food offering with a pleasing aroma to the Lord." This is a rather graphic description of how people in the Old Testament went about being forgiven, yet the book of Leviticus is there if for no other reason than to help us understand what it means for Jesus to be the Lamb of God — to be the sacrificial lamb.

TWO PRINCIPLES

There are at least two principles in this passage of Leviticus that come directly into John the Baptist's pronouncement. For the first principle, as we look at Leviticus, we understand that sin against the holy God is a serious thing; that's very clear. It is something that is punishable by death. We can just imagine going to the altar and slitting the animal's throat and then hacking its body into pieces; we can understand how that would send a pretty strong message. Sin is really, really bad, and punishable by death.

The second principle that comes out of Leviticus, which is just as important, is that God is a merciful God. As a merciful God, he will accept the death of a sinless substitute in place of the sinner, and he will forgive our sin. Sin is so horrible and vile that it requires death, but God, in his mercy, will accept the death of a sinless substitute in our place; these two principles help us understand what it means for Jesus to be the sacrificial Lamb of God.

It means that we understand that our sin must be punished. As Paul tells the Roman church, "The wages of sin is death." As well, we also understand that God, in his mercy, will accept the death of Jesus in our place; that is why theologians sometimes will call it the "substitutionary atonement." Atonement is what Jesus accomplished on the cross, and it was accomplished by his being our substitute, his being our sinless sacrifice, substituting for our own death.

This is what the prophet Isaiah was talking about in Isaiah 53, some 700 years before the time of Christ. Isaiah knew that Jesus was coming and he knew that Jesus was going to die. He knew that Jesus was going to die as a substitute for our sin, and so he writes in Isaiah 53:5, "But he," Jesus, "was wounded for our transgressions; he was crushed for our iniquities; upon him was the chastisement that brought us peace, and with his stripes we are healed. All we like sheep have gone astray; we have turned — every one — to his own way; and the Lord," God the Father, "has laid on him," Jesus, "the iniquity of us all."

Jesus is the Lamb of God; our sin requires death, but God, in his mercy, allows the substitution of a sinless sacrifice to pay the penalty for our sin, and that is why John the Baptist continues, "Behold the Lamb of God who takes away the sin of the world." On the cross, God took our sin away from us and laid it on Jesus.

Paul tells the Corinthians, "he who knew no sin was made to be sin so that you and I could be made the righteousness of God." Our sin was taken away from us and laid on Jesus. He was made to be sin because he had lived a sinless life, and therefore, his sacrifice was perfect for our sin.

TWO RAMIFICATIONS

I know that this is somewhat of a review because we talked about issues of conversion when we started this series. However, there are two ramifications that are important to focus on when we think about Jesus' being the Lamb of God, who takes away the sin of the world.

1. "Lamb of God who takes away"

The first of those ramifications is that only the Lamb of God can take away sin. Jesus, and Jesus alone, is the acceptable sacrifice to pay the penalty for our sin. Sin is not taken away by being a good Muslim. Sin is not taken away by being a good Hindu. Sin is not taken away by being a good Buddhist or a Baptist. Sin is not taken away by being a nice person or being a religious person. Sin is not taken away by doing certain things like attending church or confessing to a priest or being baptized.

Sin can only be removed by the Lamb of God, because only the Lamb of God was the sinless, substitutionary sacrifice for my sin and your sin. Jesus says, "I am the Way and the Truth and the Life. No one comes to the Father but by me." Peter says in Acts 4, "There is salvation in no one else, for there's no other name under heaven given among men whereby we must be saved." Jesus is the only Lamb of God and only the Lamb of God can take away sin.

This notion of absolute claim to uniqueness and being exclusive is absolutely central and non-negotiable in our sharing of the Gospel, and it runs totally contrary to American culture. This notion doesn't run contrary to a lot of other cultures, but it runs contrary to our culture. As new Christians, we are going to start running up against this pretty soon, if we haven't already. What our friends and co-workers will tell us is that there really is no such thing as absolute truth. They'll say, "There's nothing really right or really wrong." "There's nothing that's really true or really false." "Everything is relative." "Your truth is just as valid as my truth, and that's okay because, in fact, my truth may change between this morning and this afternoon. It's okay because there's no such thing as absolute truth."

So look at them and pray a prayer and say, "No, there is only one way for sin to be forgiven because there is only one Lamb of God. There is only one Lamb of God who took away the sin of the world." We will be told that all roads lead to heaven. Our answer is "No, all roads except one lead to hell." Our answer is not because we're arrogant, but because there was only one Lamb of God, only one God-man who did something about sin, and only one acceptable sacrifice; there is only one way for sin to be taken away. Only the Lamb of God can take away sin.

2. "The sin of the world"

The second ramification is wrapped up in the phrase, "the

sin of the world." "Behold the Lamb of God who takes away the sin of the world." The Lamb of God takes away all of the sin of the entire world. John tells us in his letter that Jesus is the propitiation — or as the NIV translates it, the atoning sacrifice — for our sin, and not for ours only but also for the sin of the entire world. Jesus' death is sufficient, and that's the important word. Jesus' death is sufficient to cover all of the sin for all of the world; for all who ask for forgiveness will receive.

SUFFICIENCY OF THE CROSS

The theological phrase for this important concept is the "sufficiency of the cross." The doctrine of the sufficiency of the cross is that Jesus' work on the cross is sufficient to take away the sin of all who believe. To put a different emphasis on it: Jesus did everything that needs to be done in order to remove our sin. Jesus does not need our help; he does not need the help of priests; he does not need the help of the church. Jesus' work on the cross was sufficient, and he provided the sacrifice that is sufficient to cover the sin of all who will but ask for forgiveness.

It is finished!

This doctrine of the sufficiency of the cross is powerfully illustrated at least two different ways in Scripture. The first way in which it is illustrated is Jesus' final words from the cross. As Jesus bore the penalty for our sin, actually as he bore our sin, as he was made to be sin, we believe the presence of God the Father left him for the first time in all eternity. On the cross, he cried out, "My God, my God, why have you forsaken me?" "When is this going to be over?" "When will I have paid the penalty for all this sin?" When he realized that he had paid the penalty, when he realized that it was over, he cried out, "It is finished!" Then he bowed his head and he died.

You see, when Jesus said, "It is finished," he meant exactly what he said: It is finished. If we were to ask him, "Jesus, what's finished?" He would have answered, "The work that my Father sent me to do is finished." If we were to ask him,

"What was the work you were sent to do," he could respond as back in John 6:40, "For this is the will of my Father, that everyone who looks on the Son and believes in him should have eternal life, and I will raise him up on the last day." When Jesus cried out, "It is finished," he was saying, "my work is sufficient so that to everyone who believes on me, I will grant them eternal life. Everyone who believes on me will be raised up on that final Day of Judgment to spend eternity with our Father and our brothers and sisters in heaven. It is finished! I have done what only I can do and I have done everything that I need to do; such that if you believe in me, your sin can be forgiven." It's a powerful statement.

Temple veil torn in two

The other illustration of the sufficiency of the cross, and I think my favorite, is the fact that the temple veil (the curtain) was torn in two when Jesus died. There is an area in the temple called the Holy of Holies; it's the place where God's presence used to dwell, and it was a very holy place. It was a place that only the High Priest could go in, and he could only go once a year, because he was going into the very presence of God. We know from secular sources that there was about a six-inch thick curtain that separated the Holy of Holies from the rest of the Temple. The curtain was incredibly important because it represented the presence of God on the other side of the curtain, and it represented our separation from God as we stood on this side of the curtain could not go directly into the presence of God the Father.

When Jesus died, his death was sufficient to take away the sin of the world; it was sufficient to guarantee direct access into God the Father. To make that clear, God ripped the curtain in two, from top to bottom, from his side to ours. We can now move directly into the presence of God because Jesus has done everything that was necessary to grant us full forgiveness of our sin, which enables us to come fully into the presence of God.

That curtain was torn from top to bottom; there was no partial tear — it was torn all the way. Why? Jesus' death was sufficient to take away the sin of the entire world.

Sew the curtain back up

One of the sad commentaries on human life is that religion has been busy, ever since, trying to sew that curtain back up. So many times religion says, "Jesus' death wasn't sufficient; he didn't quite do enough, and we have to help him if, in fact, we are to be forgiven and come into the presence of God." So religion likes to add on religious activity to salvation. "If we just do some things to earn God's favor — perhaps go out enough and knock on doors and witness to Jehovah — then somehow we will have finished ripping the curtain and have forgiveness of sin."

I heard a man speak who had knocked on over 70,000 doors witnessing for Jehovah and then he became a Christian. He said the problem was, "on how many doors do I have to knock; maybe it was 71,000!" So you see, he didn't believe that Jesus' death was sufficient and so he had to give God a helping hand by earning favor; by doing religious things; by witnessing for Jehovah — sewing up that curtain as fast as he could. Other parts of religion will tell you, "No. You can't come into the presence of God." "That Temple curtain isn't totally torn." "If you were going to confess your sin, you don't confess them to God, you confess them to a priest." "Certainly you can't come into the presence of God."

Even worse still, some religion teaches that the cross wasn't sufficient; that Jesus' death was not sufficient, and therefore, we have to keep killing Jesus every day in Mass. My nephew who serves at Mass will say, "Time to go to the sacrifice." He understands very clearly that they think they are killing Jesus every celebration of Mass.

These are all ways in which, frankly, we thumb our noses at the work of Christ. We say, "No, you did not take away the sin of the world." "No, your work on the cross was not sufficient to guarantee me forgiveness and full access to God."

The Bible says that Jesus died as the Lamb of God; he and he alone takes away the sin of the world — there is forgiveness of sin in no one or nothing else; Jesus did all that needed to be done. His work on the cross is sufficient to take away the sin of the entire world. This truth is just as true for us now as it was when we first believed. When presenting the Gospel, it's important that people understand that the only way to the Father is through the Son. When we're coming up to the point of conversion, it's important that we understand "Jesus paid it all, and all to him I owe," as the songwriter says.

As life continues, we're tempted to forget the uniqueness and the sufficiency of the cross, but that truth is still as true for us who are children of God. There is a temptation to think, "Yes, I became a Christian through the work of Jesus on the cross, but there's other ways to get there; other ways to have sin forgiven." As we move along in our Christian walk, we can easily think that God needs a helping hand. However, the cross is sufficient, both in conversion and in our walk as Christians, and we must never leave the hope to which we originally grasped — that "Jesus paid it all, and all to him I owe." That's the doctrine of that atonement — what Jesus did on the cross — but the atonement does no good unless we respond to it.

WE MUST RESPOND TO THE ATONEMENT

We are not universalists; we do not believe that Jesus' death paid the penalty for all people, so all people automatically go to heaven; that's never been Christian doctrine. Christian doctrine has always required that we respond to the message of the cross, and that we respond to the atonement. John 6:40 says, "For this is the will of my Father, that everyone who looks on the Son *and believes in him* may have eternal life."

When Peter was preaching his great sermon in Acts 2, and they came to him saying, "What must we do to be saved?" He didn't say, "Nothing! Jesus paid the price of everyone's sin, so everyone automatically goes to heaven." Peter did not say that. He said, "you must respond to the good news of Jesus Christ on the cross; you must repent and be baptized.

Paul tells the Ephesian church, "For by grace you have been saved through faith." Grace is God's gracious gift of the Lamb, and faith is our necessary response; our believing that Jesus was the Lamb of God; our believing that he and he alone sufficiently paid the penalty of our sin. Conversion is such a crucial step. Conversion is absolutely crucial because no one is born a Christian. No one who was baptized as an infant automatically goes to heaven. My mom was a relatively young Christian when I was born and the hospital wanted to baptize me; they were insistent. Mom had to threaten to sue them if one drop of water touched her baby's head, because being baptized as an infant doesn't do anything but confuse people. There is no family plan; no one goes to heaven because of his mom or dad or his brothers or sisters or his uncles or great-aunts. Every one of us must respond to the message of the atonement for the forgiveness of sin to be applied to you and to me.

COMMUNION

There is a wonderful teaching tool in scripture as we perhaps struggle to understand the immensity of the atonement; it's also a good tool that reminds us all about what the atonement is. That teaching tool is Communion. Some churches have other names for it: some call it the Lord's Supper, and some call it Eucharist — just different words to describe the same thing. Communion is a ritual; it's one of the two rituals that Jesus gave us — he gave us baptism and he gave us communion. Communion is a good ritual, and it's one of those good rituals because it's there to teach us, as well as to remind us, about the nature of the atonement.

Egypt, 1400 BC

When the Jewish nation was enslaved in Egypt around 1400 BC, God saved his chosen people through a series of plagues, which became known as the Exodus — the going out of Israel, out of slavery and out of Egypt. The Jews rightly look back at the Exodus as the greatest salvation act in the history of reality. We read in the book of Exodus 12, the instructions that God gave his children to get ready for the tenth plague, the most horrible plague. I'm going to skip around a bit, but these are the instructions starting in Exodus 12:3."

Take a lamb according to their fathers' houses, a lamb for a household. And if the household is too small for a lamb, then he and his nearest neighbor shall take according to the number of persons," they wanted to make sure that there were enough people to eat the whole lamb, "according to what each can eat you shall make your count for the lamb." It was a family affair; they got a group of people together.

Now verse 6. "The whole assembly of the congregation of Israel shall kill their lambs at twilight. Then they shall take some of the blood and put it on the two door posts and the lintel of the houses," the area over the top of the door, "in which they eat it. They shall eat the flesh that night, roasted on the fire; with unleavened bread and bitter herbs they shall eat it." The unleavened bread was symbolic of the fact that God was going to save them quickly; there wasn't even time for the bread to rise. The bitter herbs are there to remind them of their bitter years of slavery in Egypt.

Verse 11 goes on to say, "In this manner you shall eat it: with your belt fastened, your sandals on your feet, and your staff in your hand. And you shall eat it in haste. It is the Lord's Passover. For I will pass through the land of Egypt that night, and I will strike all the firstborn in the land of Egypt, both man and beast; and on all the gods of Egypt I will execute judgments: I am the Lord." Verse 13, "The blood shall be a sign for you, on the houses where you are. And when I see the blood, I will pass over you, and no plague will befall you to destroy you, when I strike the land of Egypt."

As the instructions continue, God makes it clear that this was to be a yearly festival, a yearly celebration of the salvation of the Lord. Among other things, it was to continue to be a family time of instruction. Verse 25 says, "And when you come to the land that the Lord will give you," the Promised Land, Canaan, "as he has promised, you shall keep this service," this yearly festival. "And when your children say to you, 'What do you mean by this service?' You shall say to them, 'It is the sacrifice of the Lord's Passover, for he passed over the houses of the people of Israel in Egypt, when he struck the Egyptians but spared our houses.'"

Jesus Reinterprets Passover

That's the background to the story of Passover. On the night that Jesus was betrayed, it was that Passover meal that they were celebrating together. It's interesting as Paul writes to the Corinthian church in 1 Corinthians 11 that as Jesus was celebrating the Passover, he was reinterpreting the Passover.

Jesus was reinterpreting the Passover in a way that the Passover meal, now what we call Communion, would be this teaching tool to help us understand the atonement.

Paul says in 1 Corinthians 11:23-26, "For I received from the Lord what I also delivered to you, that the Lord Jesus on the night when he was betrayed took bread, and when he had given thanks, he broke it, and said, 'This is my body, which is for you; do this in remembrance of me.' In the same way also he took the cup, after supper, saying, 'This cup is the new covenant in my blood. Do this, as often as you drink it, in remembrance of me.' For as often as you eat this bread and drink the cup, you proclaim the Lord's death until he comes." Jesus is reinterpreting the Passover meal and he's saying that the cross is now the greatest act of God's salvation. The Passover bread now points to Jesus' death, Jesus' body broken on the cross.

When Jesus says, "this is my body and this is my blood," we don't believe that it literally becomes flesh and blood. We believe that the elements, as we call them, represent Christ's body and Christ's death. Sometimes we use unleavened bread in reflection on the historical antecedents of Communion. Sometimes we use crackers that break, and sometimes we use bread that tears — they are all ways to help us understand that this stands for Christ's body, which was broken and torn on the cross for you and for me. The Passover Cup now points to Jesus' death, his blood shed on the cross; it is why we use a dark liquid and not a light liquid. The dark liquid helps us remember Christ's blood — the blood of the Lamb of God, who died for you and me as a substitution to pay the penalty for your sin and mine.

Jesus is the Lamb of God. He's the only one who ever died for your sin and mine. His death is sufficient to cover all of your sin and mine; all of the sin of all who believe and will come to him. The Gospel is good news indeed, is it not?

9

Learning More about the Holy Spirit

In the past, we have talked about the fact that Christians are monotheists; we believe in one God. Our being monotheists, for example, is why Jesus can say to Philip, "If you've seen me, you've seen the Father." And, "I and the Father are one." We are also Trinitarians; we believe, as theologians say, in the three persons of the Godhead. We believe that God the Father is fully God and distinct from God the Son; and likewise, we believe that God the Son, Jesus, is fully God and distinct from the Father. We also believe in God the Holy Spirit. God the Holy Spirit is fully God and yet distinct from God the Father and distinct from God the Son.

We're monotheists and we are Trinitarians; this is heavy-duty theology, but it's why Jesus can tell us, "Go make disciples, baptizing them in the name" (singular) "of the Father and the Son and the Holy Spirit." We admit that this theology is a mystery, but we believe it because the Bible teaches it, and we're not surprised because we know we cannot fully understand the person of God.

What I would like to do is focus our attention on the activity of the third member of the Trinity. I want to look specifically at two of his primary tasks: the Holy Spirit regenerates and the Holy Spirit Indwells.

THE HOLY SPIRIT REGENERATES

First, the Holy Spirit is the agent of regeneration. Regeneration is defined simply as the process by which God gives us new life. God gives us new birth, and he makes us into a new creation; that's what regeneration means — the actual point in time in our conversion in which we are made alive. The process of regeneration is the specific responsibility of the Holy Spirit — he's the agent of regeneration.

The process of regeneration begins, for many of us, years before we actually become Christians; the process begins when we are convicted of our sin. In John 16:7-8, Jesus says, "Nevertheless, I tell you the truth: it is to your advantage that I go away" (he's preparing the disciples for his death and ascension into heaven), "for if I do not go away, the helper will not come to you. But if I go, I will send him to you. And when he comes, he will convict the world concerning sin and righteousness and judgment." "World" here means non-believers, and part of the Holy Spirit's function is to show the world (non-believers) their sin, and then he shows them God's righteousness. He then proclaims God's coming judgment because they are sinful and God is righteous. All of this is part of the function of the Holy Spirit.

Do you remember when you first became aware that something was wrong? That something was missing? That there was emptiness in your life? Our awareness was the work of the Holy Spirit, who was convicting us of our sin; in the midst of that conviction, the Holy Spirit starts to draw us to God. Do you remember when Jesus said, "No one can come to me unless the Father who sent me draws him?" (John 6:44). The Father draws people to himself through the work of the third member of the Trinity — the Holy Spirit. Do you remember that first time you found yourself believing, "Maybe there is something to this Jesus stuff"? That was the Holy Spirit in the midst of his conviction of our sin, drawing us to the person and the claims of Jesus Christ — drawing us to God.

Then the Holy Spirit does the actual work of regeneration in our lives. The Holy Spirit is the one who gives us new life and new birth. In John 3:5, Jesus talked with Nicodemus saying, "Jesus answered, 'Truly, truly, I say to you, unless one is born of water and the Spirit" (capital "S"), "he cannot enter the kingdom of God.'" The Holy Spirit's job is to come in, to cleanse, and then to renew — to regenerate and give us life. The Holy Spirit is the agent of regeneration.

Paul says the same thing in Titus 3:4-6: "But when the

goodness and loving kindness of God our Savior appeared, he saved us, not because of works done by us in righteousness, but according to his own mercy." Then Paul continues by saying how God the Father went about saving us: "by the washing of regeneration and renewal of the Holy Spirit, whom he poured out on us richly through Jesus Christ our Savior." Titus 3:4-6 is one of the really important Trinitarian passages in the entire Bible — it was God the Father who decided that he would save his people. He saved his people through what God the Son did on the cross, which enabled God the Spirit to come and to wash us clean and to regenerate our hearts. The Holy Spirit is the agent of regeneration, and it is he who comes in and makes us new.

The Holy Spirit doesn't stop at being the agent of regeneration, but he is also the seal of our regeneration. What happens when we seal a document? We let a little wax drop on the document and then we stick our ring into the wax. (We don't do it this way much anymore.) What we're doing are two things to the document. (1) We're marking ownership because it's our seal, and (2) we're protecting the document — the seal is going to keep the scroll rolled up or the book shut. The Holy Spirit is doing the same thing: he is the seal of our inheritance; he is God's mark of ownership on our lives — The Holy Spirit is our protector.

What we have just discussed is what Paul is talking about in Ephesians 1:13-14. "In him" (Jesus) "you also, when you heard the word of truth, the Gospel of your salvation, and believed in him," (you) "were sealed with the promised Holy Spirit, who is the guarantee of our inheritance until we acquire possession of it, to the praise of his glory." When you and I became Christians, finally through the regenerating work of the Holy Spirit in our lives, he put God's stamp of ownership on us and he protected us. The Holy Spirit is keeping us safe (guaranteeing our inheritance), which Peter tells us is "kept for us in heaven," and that inheritance is kept safe until we die and go home.

In Modern Greek, the word "seal" is now used of a wedding ring. In order for this illustration to have its force, we're going to have to go back to older customs where the engagement was the legally binding ceremony. In that day and age, if we were going to break an engagement, we would have to get a divorce, which is not like today. The Holy Spirit comes and he seals us; he is our engagement ring that guarantees our marriage with the Lamb when we go to heaven.

The Holy Spirit regenerates us, convicts us of our sin, draws us to God, makes us into new people, and then he seals us — protecting our inheritance and us until we go home to heaven. Where would we be without the Holy Spirit? I'll tell you where we'd be: We would be dead in our sin, unable to respond to God — we would be guaranteed only of hell. Thanks be' to God for his unspeakable gift of the Holy Spirit to us.

THE HOLY SPIRIT INDWELLS

Second, the Holy Spirit indwells us — we tend to use the words, "The indwelling of the Holy Spirit." In John 14, Jesus is getting his disciples ready because he knows he's going to die and leave them. Jesus says in John 14:16, "And I will ask the Father, and he will give you another helper, to be with you forever, even the Spirit of truth, whom the world cannot receive, because it neither sees him nor knows him. You know him, for he dwells with you and will be in you." Jesus is the disciples' helper, but he has to leave, and so God the Father is going to send another helper, another person, who is going to be like Jesus; except in this case, this helper will never leave as was required of Jesus.

We may have heard of the word Paraclete, which is the Greek word that is translated here with "helper." Paraclete literally means someone who comes alongside. The idea is that the Paraclete comes alongside to help us; we don't really have an English word that matches up with this, so sometimes we translate it as "helper" or "comforter" or "advocate" — sometimes we give up and call him the "Paraclete." Jesus is talking about the Holy Spirit, who at Pentecost in Acts 2 came and fully indwelt all believers; the same Holy Spirit that comes upon you and me in our conversion.

The Holy Spirit doesn't just come and regenerate us and leave, but rather he comes and regenerates us, makes us new, and stays; he stays with us and in us — he is within and indwelling each one of us. Jesus isn't talking about some kind of divine impersonal force; that is not what he is. The Holy Spirit is God just as much as the Father is God and just as much as the Son is God; he is as personal as God the Father is. We relate to him as a person in the same way that we relate to God the Son. God the Spirit is fully God and he is personally involved in every aspect of our daily lives.

The Holy Spirit is involved with each one of us because he is here to help and come alongside each one of us. The Holy Spirit helps in many ways. As we read through the Bible and receive the work of the Holy Spirit, we'll see, among other things, that the Holy Spirit assures us that we are the children of God. He whispers to us from the inside that we belong to God. He helps us in our prayers when we don't know how to pray. He searches the depths of our hearts deeper than words can go and expresses the deep longings of our hearts to God; that's not a charismatic gift, but it's something true of all believers (Romans 8). The Holy Spirit also guarantees our final resurrection, and the list goes on, but his primary work, or at least his daily work, is guiding and empowering us.

The Holy Spirit indwells us in order to guide and empower us. Daily the Holy Spirit guides each one of us. The Bible talks about our being led by the Spirit, and sometimes it talks about walking in the Spirit or walking by the Spirit. "But I say, walk by the Spirit, and you will not gratify the desires of the flesh" (Galatians 5:16). Paul says to walk in accordance with the Spirit; that is how he is guiding us.

The Holy Spirit guides us in different ways. The main way in which the Holy Spirit guides us is through the Bible. As we read the Bible, he helps us to understand what it means, and he helps us apply it in our lives. In writing the second letter to Timothy, Paul gives him some pretty difficult things to understand and then says, "Think over what I say, for the Lord will give you understanding in everything" (2 Timothy 2:7). Part of the Holy Spirit's function is that as we read our Bibles, which is the word of God, he is at work in our minds to help us understand and apply the Word; it is so we can say, "Yeah, I'm talking about you in verse 4." "Yes, this is for you, Bill — get it through your head!"

The Holy Spirit also guides us, I think, by speaking to us.

We have to be careful here because anything that we think the Holy Spirit is saying in our heads must parallel to what the Bible says. I don't know how many times I've talked to people who say, "The Lord is leading me to do this." I say, "No, he's not because the Lord never leads in a way that is contrary to Scripture." "I just really feel that God wants me to divorce my husband or wife"; this is one of the more common excuses for divorce. No, that voice isn't God's; it's Satan's because God's voice in our heads will never contradict the Bible, never! Yet with that caveat, I believe that the Holy Spirit is also working inside of us and guiding us by reminding us — he is pointing out things to us.

About a year ago, I started asking God if he would give his Spirit an accent! "God, there are a lot of voices floating in my head: there's me, there's my sinful nature, and there's my baggage from past experiences. I know that the Holy Spirit is in there and he's trying to get my attention, but I struggle sometimes to know which voice is his. Could you give him an accent like a nice North Carolina drawl? That would be nice!" This whole concept about being guided by the Spirit is a process; it's not something that happens instantly over-night. Yet it has been remarkable, because as I try to listen and distinguish voices in my head, I think I'm coming to hear the Spirit's accent. Normally, he is saying, "Shut up, Bill, you don't need to say that so keep it quiet." I think that's one of the ways in which the Spirit guides us.

The Holy Spirit never guides us in a way that is contrary to Scripture. The Holy Spirit is that voice in our heads who takes Scripture, things we know, experiences in our lives, and conversations we have with our non-Christian friends, and he says, "Push that point." "Talk to them a little more." "Ask him about his spouse." "Ask him about his kids." "Find out what's going on in his life."

The Holy Spirit is working in our hearts and minds from the inside out, guiding us daily; it's how we walk by the Spirit. The Holy Spirit also enables us not only to hear his voice, but then he gives us the power to do what that voice is saying — the Holy Spirit empowers us daily.

One of my favorite passages is Philippians 2:12-13, where Paul tells the Philippian church, "Therefore, my beloved, as you have always obeyed, so now, not only as in my presence but much more in my absence, work out your own salvation with fear and trembling, for it is God who works in you, both to will and to work for his good pleasure." J.B. Phillips' translation helps us understand Paul's theology a little bit better. He writes, "Be keener than ever to work out the salvation that God has given you with a proper sense of awe and responsibility, for it is God who is at work within you, giving you the will and the power to achieve his purpose."

God the Holy Spirit is at work in you and me, planting desires in our hearts, and then giving us the power to enable us to actually accomplish what is in our hearts. I want to say some things about empowerment because this is one of those issues that can be kind of confusing and frustrating at times; it would be easy to be a legalist at this point. "Wow, you know, you just have to conform your outside behavior to what God commands and that's all that matters"; legalism is easy in that sense. However, the Holy Spirit indwells us and he works from the inside out; he works from our hearts to our mouths to our hands and to our feet. What we need to do as Christians is to learn not only to hear the Holy Spirit, but also allow his power to accomplish his work in our lives.

SPIRITUAL GIFTS

One of the ways in which God empowers us is certainly through the gifts that he's given us. I'm talking about the issue of what is called "spiritual gifts." The Bible teaches that every one of us was given at least one supernatural gift when we became Christians. If you're a new Christian, you may not be aware that you now have a supernatural gift through the power of the Spirit residing in you. Sometimes God's gifts parallel our natural gifts (of course there is no such thing as "natural" gifts because God controlled how our genes went together), but sometimes the spiritual gifts are kind of an enhancement of what we're already doing. Sometimes our spiritual gift is radically different than what we naturally are able to do, but every one of us, as Christians, has at least one.

There are places in the Bible that list many gifts that include gifts of teaching, preaching, evangelizing, serving, and encouraging, or being a pastor or administrator. The Bible also lists the gift of giving, which is a supernatural ability to make unusual amounts of money paralleled by a really deep conviction that we are God's stewards to use his wealth for his purposes — it's a gift to make money and equally a gift to give it away. Other gifts listed in the Bible are gifts of leading the church, mercy, wisdom, healing, and doing miracles.

There are probably many more gifts than those listed in the Bible, but the Spirit has this wide variety of gifts that he gives to his church because there are a wide variety of needs in the church. To meet the needs of the body, he gifts all the members of the body so that all of us can be involved in the lives of the body of Christ, using our gifts for the service of the church. Paul explicitly says in 1 Corinthians 12:7, "To each is given the manifestation of the Spirit for the common good." The gifts we have are to be used for the common good of the church. Peter says we are to use our gifts to serve one another as stewards of God's grace. One way in which the Holy Spirit empowers us is to give us a wide variety of gifts to meet the wide variety of needs in the church.

Under the general category of empowerment, we also ask about purpose: "What is the purpose of the Holy Spirit's guiding us and empowering us?" The purpose is that our lives change; that's the whole point. Do we want to know what the will of God is? The will of God is our sanctification; it's our holiness — Paul tells that to the Thessalonian church. There, we don't have to ask that question any more! What's God's will for our lives? God's will or our lives is for us to be holy; it is for our lives to change; it is to look more like Jesus Christ; everything else is commentary.

FRUITS OF THE SPIRIT

Paul tells the Romans and us that the good God is going to work in our lives is so that we are conformed to the image of his Son; that you and I look more and more like Jesus. "For those whom he foreknew he also predestined to be conformed to the image of his Son, in order that he might be the firstborn among many brothers" (Romans 8:29). Paul tells the Corinthians that we are being changed from one degree of glory into the next.

John tells us, "Beloved, we are God's children now, and what we will be has not yet appeared; but we know that when he appears we shall be like him, because we shall see him as he is" (1 John 3:2). 1 John 3:2 is God's goal for our lives, and that's why the Spirit is guiding us and that's why the Spirit is empowering us — because he wants our lives to exhibit what are called the "Fruits of the Spirit." Jesus told his disciples, "By this my Father is glorified that you bear much fruit and so prove to be my disciples." Fruit simply means the visible results of our having our lives changed — the visible results are called fruit.

The main passage on fruits is in Galatians 5. Paul starts in verse 16 where he says, "But I say, 'Walk by the Spirit, and you will not gratify the desires of the flesh.'" Walk by the guidance of the Spirit; walk by the power that the Spirit gives us. If we do that, we're not going to accomplish the desires of the flesh. Then he sets up a contrast between the desires of the flesh and the fruits of the Spirit. Paul says, "Now the works of the flesh are evident: sexual immorality, impurity, sensuality, idolatry, sorcery, enmity, strife, jealousy, fits of anger, rivalries, dissensions, divisions, envy, drunkenness, orgies, and things like these. I warn you, as I warned you before, that those who do such things will not inherit the kingdom of God. But the fruit of the Spirit is love, joy, peace, patience, kindness, goodness, faithfulness, gentleness, self-control; against such things there is no law. And those who belong to Christ Jesus have crucified the flesh with its passions and desires. If we live by the Spirit, let us also walk by the Spirit."

If the Spirit has given us regenerated lives, then the lives that follow out must be lived by the Spirit; of walking in the Spirit; of listening to his guidance and allowing his power to help us accomplish the work that he's given us. "Let us not become conceited, provoking one another, envying one another." The purpose of the Holy Spirit's guidance and the purpose of the Holy Spirit's empowerment is so our lives will change and start to show love and joy where there was neither love nor joy.

The interesting thing is that the Holy Spirit will not empower us or produce fruit in us without our cooperation;

we don't cooperate in our salvation, but we do cooperate in our sanctification. The whole business of growth into holiness is not some automatic thing where we can sit back and say, "Whatever!" We can actually fight against the Spirit; the Bible calls it quenching the Spirit or grieving the Spirit. In Hebrews, the author talks about a person outraging the Holy Spirit; this happens when we hear the Spirit but we do not listen; this happens when we are prompted to obey and yet we disobey. We can fight the work of God's Spirit, and when we do, what happens? The Holy Spirit starts to withdraw the blessings of God in our lives, and he will start to exert corrective discipline. Paul tells the Corinthians that many of them have become sick and some have even died because they defiled the Lord's Supper, they ridiculed the poor, and they ridiculed the cross. The Holy Spirit became angry with them and so some were made to be sick and some were simply taken home to heaven. How much better it is to hear and listen to the Holy Spirit! How much better it is to be prompted and to obey the Holy Spirit!

WHAT DOES IT LOOK LIKE TO BE EMPOWERED?

Finally, we are at a very practical level: What does it look like to be empowered? This is a very difficult question. Paul tells the Philippians that God is at work in us, giving us desires; we understand that, but then he gives us the power to accomplish those desires. We might ask, "How is that different from putting my nose to a grindstone and working really hard? What does it look like to have this balance?" These are hard questions to even answer.

What does it look like to allow God's Spirit to enable us to accomplish the work that he has given us to do? Whether it's preaching or growth in holiness, how do we let the Spirit do that? I have no idea; it's a mystical concept. When it happens, we'll know it though. All of the sudden, we will look at our lives and realize, "My goodness, I don't hate him anymore. How did that happen? I couldn't do that on my own." The Holy Spirit is at work.

So when it happens, we'll know it. The question is: "What does it look like?" There's much I don't understand, but there are a couple of things about which I have a pretty clear idea. Allowing the Spirit's power to flow through us and allowing him to be the strength and the enablement for us to move forward begins with our confession of saying, "I can't"; it has to begin there. When we look at someone we hate or someone with whom we're angry — or the whole issue of growing in holiness — growth starts by saying, "God, I can't do that; I can't love that person anymore." "God, I can't stop gossiping on my own; I've done it all my life! I open my mouth, and out it flows; I can't stop it."

Confession is the first step toward recovering. Have we not noticed over and over again, how many times in the Psalms where the writers say, "Oh God, you are my rock and my helper, in you I trust?" The Psalmist understood when he said, "I can't take care of my enemies." "I can't do what you've called me to do on my own. It's you that's going to do it." Even David, a thousand years before the full outpouring of the Holy Spirit, understood that the enablement of God in our lives begins by saying, "I can't do it," and then followed by faith in God's ability to do it.

I cannot do anything in a sermon to change our hearts. I can't do anything by preaching to make us more like Jesus Christ. Do you know what? I know that — there is nothing I can do. There's certainly nothing that programs can do or elders can do to change our hearts and we admit that.

However, we do believe with every fiber in our beings that God can — it's my prayer every Sunday before I stand up here. So the process is to turn you and me over to the working of the Holy Spirit. Zechariah says, "'It's not by might, it's not by power, but it's by my Spirit,' says the Lord." Not because of my power, but it's because of the Spirit of God who is at work in the midst of his children, guiding them and empowering them; that's how this work gets done, and that's how lives are changed; not because we're strong.

Don't ever think we can just sit back and let God do it all; this is not an excuse for laziness. I will never stand before you and try to deliver some sort of spiritual stream of consciousness because I was too lazy to study the preceding week. In Romans 12:1-2, it is interesting when Paul says, "I appeal to you therefore, brothers, by the mercies of God, to present your bodies as a living sacrifice, holy and acceptable to God, which is your spiritual worship. Do not be conformed to this world, but be transformed by the renewal of your mind, that by testing you may discern what is the will of God, what is good and acceptable and perfect."

There is no place for us to say, "Whatever! God's going to do his work"; that's not the way it works. However, it does begin by saying, "God, I can't do it, but I believe through the power of your Spirit, you can make me look like Jesus. So by your guidance and strength, I will present my whole body, everything that I am, to you as a living sacrifice. I will, as your Spirit enables me, not let the world squeeze me into its mold."

Where would we be without the indwelling of the Holy Spirit? Where would we be without his empowerment? We'd be unable to fight sin; we'd be unable to enjoy the victory of our lives. Thanks be' to God for his unspeakable gift of the Holy Spirit.

I'll close with John 7:37-38. Jesus is in Jerusalem and he says, "On the last day of the feast, the great day, Jesus stood up and cried out, 'If anyone thirsts, let him come to me and drink. Whoever believes in me,' as the Scripture has said, 'Out of his heart will flow rivers of living water.'" Then Jesus goes on to explain that it is the Spirit that is the river of living water, the Spirit that wants to gush, to flow out of our souls and out of our lives and flood our lives and flood our families and flood our churches.

Thanks be to God for his unspeakable gift of the Holy Spirit!

10

Walking with God

SANCTIFICATION

Today, I want to talk about the whole topic of walking with God. This topic has been a very difficult talk to put together, because I didn't know where in this series to put it; if this were a series of thirty, it would have been the twenty-eighth because it's a little hard, maybe a little too much. However, it's important that over this talk, I cover all the basic fundamental issues that we as new believers need to know. So, in biblical language, "gird up your loins" (get ready) and hang in there, because we do need to talk about this whole issue of sanctification.

Sanctification is a fancy, theological term, which simply means that we are set apart from sin. Sanctification means that in our walk with God, we are to become holy. When we became Christians, we were, in a sense, babes in Christ; but just as babies are to grow into mature adulthood, so also are we to grow spiritually into spiritual maturity.

What does spiritual growth look like?

What does spiritual growth look like? Spiritual growth means that as we walk day in, day out, we look more and more like Jesus and less and less like the world. Spiritual growth means our attitudes and behavior more and more start to reflect the attitude and behavior of Jesus Christ. Our lives start to show the fruits of the Spirit; where there was no love, now there is love; where there was no joy, there is now a deep joy that looks beyond the circumstances of life, rooted in the peace we have with God because we have been reconciled.

Sanctification is the process of looking less like the world and looking more like our heavenly Father.

God's will for your life

Have you ever asked yourselves, "What is the will of God for my life?" or "What does God want me to do?" This question is the easiest question to answer! The answer is in I Thessalonians 4:3, "For this is the will of God, your sanctification." Almost everything else is just commentary. What God wants is for us, one step at a time, to look less and less like the world and more and more like his Son, Jesus Christ.

There are a lot of verses that talk about sanctification, and my favorite is Romans 12:1-2 where Paul says to the church in Rome, "I appeal to you," I urge or beg of you, "therefore, brothers, by the mercies of God, to present your bodies as a living sacrifice, holy and acceptable to God, which is your spiritual worship. Do not be conformed to this world, but be transformed by the renewal of your mind, that by testing you may discern what is the will of God, what is good and acceptable and perfect."

This is the will of God for our lives; to look at what God has done in all of his mercy in saving us, and then in response saying, "I give everything that I am to you sacrificially. My desire is not to be conformed to this world, not to allow it to squeeze me into its mold, but rather to be transformed. Not transformed by legalism or by all these rules I must follow, but to be transformed from the inside with the renewal of my mind showing itself in my walk." This is sanctification; this is what our walk with God is to look like.

GOD ALLOWS DIFFICULT CIRCUMSTANCES

The practical question of sanctification obviously is, "Have we started the process of growth into spiritual maturity?" or "Have we started to change and look less like the world and more like Jesus?" In his love and his grace and his mercy and his power and his sovereignty (he is King of Kings and Lord of Lords), this loving God allows difficult circumstances into our lives to help us grow; to help us in our walk; to help us become more like Jesus. A good, loving, all-powerful God will allow difficult circumstances into our lives.

He will allow accidents. He will allow sickness. He will allow perhaps unemployment. Then, on top of all these good things, he will allow us to be persecuted for our faith. These good things will most likely start with our friends. Our friends will look at us and say, "hey, you're different. What's wrong with you? Do you think you're better than we are? Come on, let's keep doing the things we have always done." Our friends will not understand when we say, "No, I don't want to do that anymore." Perhaps we will suffer at work; perhaps we'll be passed over for a promotion because our boss hates Christians. Perhaps our neighbors and even our family members will ostracize us because they think that we think we're better than they are and we're standing in judgment of them by being Christians. Difficult circumstances are going to come into our lives, and we know this because it comes into all Christians' lives.

What did I do wrong?

We are going to be tempted to say, "What did I do wrong? Certainly, I've done something wrong for these difficult things to happen to me." The answer from Scripture is, "No, you probably did something right, and that's why these difficult circumstances are in your life." Paul tells his friend Timothy in 2 Timothy 3:12, "Everyone who seeks to live a godly life in will be persecuted." The world hates our Master, and Jesus says that "if they hated me they are going to hate you as well."

So when these difficult things happen in our lives, whether simply because we're human beings living in a fallen world or whether it's because we're Christians, our tendency will be, "Did I do something wrong," and the answer is possibly, "No." The answer probably is that God wants to do something right in our lives, and so in his sovereignty and in his control and in his goodness, he is going to allow these difficult circumstances into our lives so we can grow in our sanctification and holiness.

We grow in the difficult times

When times are good, we rarely grow; isn't that sad but true?

When the marriage is good, the family is good, work is going smoothly, the car is not breaking down, and we still don't have to paint that side of the house yet, when things are going good, how many of us grow in our faith and trust in Jesus Christ? Not many. Yet, when times of stress and hurt and difficult challenges come, we tend to grow more and become more like Jesus Christ. That's his purpose in our lives, that we look like him.

Test our genuine faith

When these difficult times occur, there are all sorts of things that could be going on in our lives. One of the things that could be going on when difficult circumstances come is that God wants to test how genuine our faith is. Now, he knows whether or not our faith is real, but he wants us to know that our faith in Jesus Christ is rock solid. In the midst of these difficult circumstances, God wants us to be not only confident but he wants our faith to be refined — to be pure.

In 1 Peter 1:6-7, Peter describes all the wonderful things that happen to a Christian; he says, "In this you rejoice, though now for a little while, if necessary, you have been grieved by various trials, so that the tested genuineness of your faith — more precious than gold that perishes though it is tested by fire — may be found to result in praise and glory and honor at the revelation of Jesus Christ." That is part of what is going on when difficult times come into our lives; we are being purified, refined, and tested, so that we can know for sure and praise God in how we respond. We know that our faith is genuine and real.

Produce Christian character

When difficult things come into our lives, what God is sometimes doing is just trying to produce a Christian character in us. For example, in Romans 5:3 Paul says, "We rejoice in our sufferings, knowing that suffering produces endurance, and endurance produces character, and character produces hope." The Christian life is a process. I don't know of any one of us, who, when we first became Christians, could look at suffering and say, "Yeah, that's not natural, but it is supernatural!"

The Christian life is a walk, a process, and it takes one step at a time; and as we get farther down this process, this walk, we learn to rejoice in our sufferings. We don't rejoice in our sufferings because we're masochists, but we learn to rejoice in our sufferings because we know God wants to produce endurance, character, and hope in our lives and this is how it happens.

My other most favorite verses — please hear my sarcasm — regarding these things are James 1:2-4, although sometimes I feel like taking a big black magic marker and crossing them out (I haven't yet). James says: "Count it all joy, my brothers, when you meet trials of various kinds" — I'm running for the hills! "No, count it all joy, Bill" — "for you know that the testing of your faith produces steadfastness. And let steadfastness have its full effect, that you may be perfect and complete, lacking in nothing." God's will for your life and mine is not the avoidance of pain, but it is his will that we look like Jesus. In his sovereign control of all things and in his love and compassion, the best way that God can get us to look like Jesus is to allow difficult circumstances to come into our lives.

God calls us to respond to these difficult circumstances not in fear but rather in faith, to listen, learn, and grow, walking the walk. This is how our faith is tested and made genuine and pure; this is how we become like Jesus. Many of you know that we lost two daughters at birth, and that's when I got the magic marker out for the first time; to get rid of these two stupid verses. I don't know how I worked through that process, but I am not who I was fifteen years ago and Robin is not who she was fifteen years ago. That was because of God's sovereign control and love and grace and mercy. God allowed difficult circumstances into my life and Robin's; in the midst, he said, "In the storms of life, hang on," and that's what we did — it means we have two more children waiting for us in heaven.

RESPONSE IS TO COMPARTMENTALIZE LIVES

When difficult situations come into our lives, the question is "How are we going to respond?" Hopefully, we will hang on for all God is worth. However, I know that temptations will come; temptations to run away and hide, temptations to not lean into the pain. We will be tempted to do anything we possibly can to get away from the pain and to make the pain go away and make it stop. One of the ways in which we will be tempted to avoid pain, among other things, is to compartmentalize our lives; I can say this because it is true of all Christians. We are tempted to divide our lives into sections and say, "God, I'm not going to give you all of myself," so we shut off doors to certain rooms in our lives. We will say, "I will give you part of my life, but I'm not going to give you that part because it's too painful and it hurts too much."

I often think of life as being a patchwork quilt, a quilt made up of many, many squares. We say, "Okay, God, these squares are yours — I will give you these squares — but other squares of my life, I will not give to you because it's too painful. I don't trust you and I don't think you have my best interests at heart, so I think I know better and I want to keep other areas of my life to myself." And life becomes this patchwork quilt.

For those of you who are new Christians, this may be a little hard to hear. I don't mean to be a prophet of doom, but you need to understand that these are the challenges that will lie ahead for your lives; perhaps you have already started to feel some twinges.

Compartmentalize time

The question is, "What's going to happen when you're tempted to compartmentalize your lives?" For example, you will be tempted to compartmentalize your time. You will be tempted to say, "This square is Sunday morning; this is the time I'm going to give to God; this is his time. However, I will keep other days and time periods for myself over here; these are different squares of the quilt. God, I've give you these squares, you should be happy with Sunday mornings, but I'm going to keep Sunday afternoon and all the time I'm at work or whatever during the week for myself because they belong to me." You are going to be tempted to compartmentalize your time.

Compartmentalize money

You will also be tempted to compartmentalize your money.

Understand that God does not need your money because it's all his, but Jesus says, "where your treasure is there your heart is also," period, end of discussion. Again, this will be a temptation: we compartmentalize our money and so we have this square over here, in the patchwork quilt of our lives, which represents our loose change; now, it's not too much so it doesn't affect our lifestyles — this is our loose change we can throw at God. "You know what, God, you should be happy." After the loose change, we keep the rest of "my money" over in other squares of our lives and say, "This money is none of your business, God." "You know, I need this money for my wealth and my portfolio so I don't have to trust you in retirement." "This money is for my bigger house." "This is for a third car even though there are only two drivers in the house."

We compartmentalize our money, forgetting, of course, it's all his. Even our bodies are his; we were bought with the precious blood of the Lamb of God and we don't own anything. We are stewards of God's wealth and we are called to use his wealth to advance his purposes. When we stand before the Judgment Seat, we will be held accountable for how we spent God's money. Yet the temptation will be to compartmentalize and say, "Okay, God, here's my loose change; the rest is mine."

Compartmentalize affections

You will also be tempted to compartmentalize your affections. You will be tempted to say, "In this situation, in this square, I'm going to love God; but in other areas of my life, he can't have my heart. I'm not going to give him my affections in these other areas. In this area of my life, he has my affections, and I'm going to go to church Sunday morning and put on a nice religious smile, and when someone says, 'How are you doing?' I will say, 'Fine.'" I think the word "fine" should be struck from the English language; it's a terrible word. "Fine" means, "My life is really lousy right now, but I'm not sure you care enough so I'm going to gloss it over." At least that's what it means in my house.

We go to church and put on the face and tell everyone we're fine and we'll also sing with smiles; however, we can't wait to get home to visit the pornography sites, to pick up those magazines, or to molest little boys and girls. I know the statistics: 50% of American males go to porn sites once a week. 25% of women are sexually molested I also know that statistically the church is no different than the world.

So we have our affections, "Oh, I love you, God," but can't wait to go home and look at naked women on the Internet. There are many areas in which you will be tempted to compartmentalize. You will be tempted to compartmentalize your tongue. "Okay, I'm going to stop using the Lord's Name in vain, and I might stop saying these couple of words, but oh, man, I'm going to keep gossiping, slandering, passing critical judgment, and devaluing people."

The temptation to compartmentalize is everywhere in our reality, and I wish this were not true. I really wish that God had done things differently; he didn't ask me, but I wish it were! I wish that when I became a Christian that sin was completely removed from my life, and that there wouldn't be these challenges or sin pulling me.

Give all to God

I wish that I could just give all of myself to God. I wish that I wouldn't shut doors to certain rooms in my heart, but that's the nature of reality; God, in his love and wisdom, saw this was the best way to do things, and he is right and I am wrong. Every time, God is right and I am wrong. This is how God has called us to grow into Christ's likeness — in difficult circumstances and challenging times. We are to open all of the doors to all of the rooms of our lives and throw away the patchwork quilt; to have one single, big square of our lives and every last bit of it is his.

I am so scared that, if you are a young Christian you will be so overwhelmed that you will run out of here saying, "Whoa, I don't want anything to do with this." But remember that this is a walk, a process, and it is something we do one step at a time. Sometimes, we will have two or three challenges, but often, at least in my life, I've noticed that God only allows one problem at a time. He says, "Okay, Bill, time to deal with this issue in your life; you didn't respond properly to that person. In fact, you tend to react too strongly to people; time for you to work on this." The worst thing we can do when these challenges come is compartmentalize them and say, "No, I'll give this to you, God, but I'm keeping these parts to myself" because that's not the deal we made.

When we became Christians, we understood that Jesus is Savior, he is Lord, he is the Boss; he is Master, and we are his disciples. Paul tells the Corinthians that we are to glorify him with anything and everything we have, including our bodies. Jesus gave all of himself to you and to me, and he expects all of us back; I think that's why he calls us followers. Jesus calls us disciples because he wants full-time, fully devoted disciples; that's the only kind of crop he wants.

In the Parable of the Four Soils, the only soil that is acceptable to the farmer is the one that produced the full crop. So also in the area of discipleship, the only thing that is acceptable to God is a fully devoted disciple of Jesus Christ; there are verses that tell us this all throughout the Bible. In what I think the is most important verse on discipleship, Jesus says, "If anyone would come after me," if anyone wants to be my follower, my disciple, a Christian, "let him deny himself and take up his cross and follow me" (Mark 8:34).

If we want to be followers of Jesus Christ, then we must deny all of our wills. We must say no to ourselves, and then everyday we are to live as those who have been crucified to our own wills. Every day we must say what Jesus said in the Garden, "Not my will but yours be done"; that's how we follow him as fully devoted disciples. Jesus also says, "So therefore, any one of you who does not renounce all that he has cannot be my disciple" (Luke 14:33). The Parable of the young Rich Ruler applies to all of us, because God demands all. Paul says in Galatians 2:20, "I have been crucified with Christ." If you want to push the metaphor, he didn't say, "I was cut by Christ," he didn't say, "I was wounded by Christ," nor "I was perhaps a little maimed by Christ," he said, "I was crucified with Christ; I died." "I have been crucified with Christ, it is no longer I who lives, but Christ who lives in me."

WHAT IF WE COMPARTMENTALIZE?

Romans 12:1-2 makes no allowance for a patchwork quilt

kind o life; it does not. Romans tells us to present our bodies and everything we are as sacrifice to God, and that means we will not look like the world but we will be transformed from the inside out; this is the challenge all of us will face, and perhaps are facing. What is going to happen if we compartmentalize our lives? What will happen if we hold back pieces of ourselves from God? What are the consequences of refusing to open all of the doors of our lives?

It will start by harming our relationship with Jesus Christ. As we sin, we will realize there is something between God and us; we will experience guilt, and guilt is a good thing; we will experience depression. As things go on and don't get better, God will start to remove his peace from our lives, and he will start to remove his blessing from our lives. Eventually, we are told that as a loving heavenly Father, God will discipline his children for their sin.

SUFFICIENCY OF THE CROSS

The amazing message of the Gospel is that because God is the God of mercy and grace, he extends his goodness to those in need and those who don't deserve it. Because of God's mercy and grace, you and I can stop this downward spiral of sin whenever we want. The wall between God and us can be removed, and the peace and blessing can come back into our lives; all we have to do is repent; all we have to do is confess. "Yes, God, once again, you're right and I'm wrong. Once again, I went my way and it was the wrong way. I am truly sorry." Because God is a God of grace, his mercy will sweep through us and remove our sin as far as the east is from the west.

Then our relationship and the peace and blessing of God will be restored; this is part of the doctrine of the sufficiency of the cross that we've talked about several times back. Jesus Christ's death on the cross was sufficient to cover all the sin of the world for all who cry out to him for forgiveness; that's true not only of the forgiveness that happened when we became Christians, but also the forgiveness for the sins we will commit as his children. No matter how much we do, and no matter how bad it is, or how many times we commit our favorite sin (we all have them, don't we?), the cross is sufficient to cover our sin.

WHAT IF WE DON'T GIVE HIM ALL?

If we go to Christ and ask for forgiveness, he will forgive our sin and the downward spiral will stop; this is where the joy and freedom is in the Christian walk. There is no joy in straddling a fence — fences were never made to be straddled. As long as we try to straddle the fence, have our patchwork-quilt life of some to God and some to us, we are going to be miserable people. However, the joy and freedom that God has promised comes when we say, "It's all yours. All of the doors are open." Unfortunately, we don't always do that.

Lose our assurance as Christians

We don't always stop the spiral; after all, there's part of us that likes to sin even as regenerated children of God. Sometimes we don't confess our sin. What will happen if sin continues in our lives, a spiral that continues to pull us farther and farther down into the muck? (Muck is a good Greek word, by the way; it is "mukaes" in the original Greek — not really.) Although generally it takes years to occur, eventually when we continue to say no to God and continue to live in our sin, we are going to lose the assurance that we are Christians — we will lose the confidence that we are children of God. Understand, "we are saved by grace through faith, and that not of ourselves; it is the gift of God." We were dead in our trespasses and sin, and not because of anything we deserve but because God is a God of mercy and grace, he plucked us from the "muckaes" of life and brought us into his eternal Kingdom. I was dead at the time; I did not help him at all.

Salvation is by grace, yet in conversion God changed us. As changed children of God, he has said that he wants our lives to change as well. The message of Scripture is if your life or my life does not continue to change, then there will come a point in which we must question whether or not we really are Christians. I will not ask you this question; I don't believe that is my job. However, through the prompting of the Holy Spirit, each one of us will have to ask ourselves the question,

"Am I really a Christian? Was my conversion real?"

Assurance does not come from a single event. Assurance of salvation isn't based on a raised hand or a prayer at camp, but rather our assurance of being a child of God, the Bible says, is all tied up with the work of the Holy Spirit in our lives. The Holy Spirit is whispering in my ears, "Yes, Bill, you are a child of God." He is saying, "Yes, Bill, you are a child of God; look at how your life is changing." The change that occurs in our lives is part of the basis of our assurance that, in fact, we are children of God. I am not making this up; it is in the Bible.

Among many passages, there is 1 John 2:3 where John says, "And by this we know that we have come to know him," this is how we know that we are in a relationship with God; that we are Christians, "if," we raise our hands at church at camp and go to church twice a year? No! That's not what it says. "We keep his commandments." There is our assurance. Keeping his commandments — not as an attempt to earn God's favor, but as the response of changed lives. "Whoever says, 'I know him,'" whoever says, "I'm a Christian," "but does not keep his commandments," has a smaller house in heaven and more menial tasks to do? Right? Wrong! "This person is a liar, and the truth is not in him," In John's vocabulary, we want the truth in us; that's the only way we get to heaven, and it's the only way to have a relationship with God. "But whoever keeps his word, in him truly the love of God is perfected." That's the changed life. Then John says again, "By this we may be sure that we are in him: whoever says he abides in him ought to walk in the same way in which he walked."

Our assurance, our absolute, rock-solid confidence, that we are children of God comes through the work of the Holy Spirit, confirming in our spirits (Romans 8) that we are children of God, showing us, "Look at your life, it's changing. Do you think you did this on your own? Do you think Satan wanted your life to change? Gee, I wonder what force in this universe is strong enough to change your heart, Bill?" There is only one strong enough to change our hearts, and it is the power of the Holy Spirit. The changes in our lives are part of our confidence that we are his children.

How terrifying it must have been to the people who went

to the church in Laodicea when they received the book of Revelation. Can you imagine getting a book written by the Apostle John and it says, "To those who go to this church..." That's what happens in Revelation. The Spirit speaks to seven churches, and to the Church of Laodicea, he says, "I know your works," I know what your life looks like, "that you are neither cold nor hot." (Cold water is good for things and hot water is good for things, but they are neither cold nor hot.) "Would that you were either cold or hot! So, because you are lukewarm, and neither hot nor cold, I will spit you out of my mouth" (Revelation 3:15-16).

So you see, there's no backseat in heaven. Often we think in terms of carnality, being a second-level Christian, but Christians in Laodicea, or people who claim they are Christians who are lukewarm, they will be spit out of his mouth. Later on in verse 19, he says, "Those whom I love, I reprove and discipline, so be zealous and repent." This is what happens when you and I like to sin; when we have our little areas of sin tucked away and we think that nobody can see them until somebody gets into the history of our Internet browser and finds out where we've been. We hang onto sin and we realize we have no confidence that we were Christians at all.

Warning passages

Wait; it gets worse! There is a whole other set of verses that we call the Warning Passages. The Warning Passages are not meant for people who are struggling and fighting the fight, or who are may be failing and confessing. The Warning Passages of Scripture are for the people who perhaps have made a profession of faith through camp, or whatever. (Don't get me wrong, I love camp.) The Warning Passages of Scripture are for the people who have this spiritual event happen in their lives where they make a profession and think they got a "Get-out-of-hell-free card," which means they think, "We can go live anyway we want, it doesn't matter." Their lives don't change and they think when they stand before the Judgment Seat of God, they can put this orange, two-and-a-half-by-three-inch card in front of his face and say, "I get out of hell free!" God will look at them and say, "What's that? I've never seen that before. Didn't you listen to my word?" It's to those kinds of people that the Warning Passages were addressed.

John 8:31 says, "If you abide in my word," if you live in me, if you walk with me, "you are truly my disciples." If we don't abide in his word, it is clear, isn't it; we are not his disciples. Jesus says that, "the one who endures to the end will be saved" (Matthew 24:13). While starting good is important, it's more important to finish well; it's the one who endures and hangs in there to the end who will be saved. Paul tells the Colossians in Colossians 1:23 that they have been reconciled and are friends with God, "if indeed you continue in the faith, stable and steadfast, not shifting from the hope of the gospel that you heard." The strongest Warning Passages are scattered all the way through the Book of Hebrews. In chapter 3:14, it says, "For we share in Christ, if indeed we hold our original confidence firm to the end."

GOD WILL ENABLE US

These are not, in one sense, pleasant verses, but they are frightening verses. Yet how can we go through a series of what the Bible says for new believers and not know there will be challenges coming? However, because God is a God of grace and mercy, he will enable us to hang in there and be steadfast and to endure. He is going to work through our difficult situations; he is going to refine our faith; he is going to confirm our faith; he is going to make us into the men and women of God he wants us to become because he wants us to look like his Son.

Our looking like his son is more important than anything else; yet in the midst of all this, we take that step. We present our bodies as a living sacrifice. We refuse, by the power of God, to be conformed to this world, but we are transformed by the renewing of our minds. When we became Christians, Jesus became our Savior, but he also became our Lord. The Boss calls us to grow up! He calls us to grow up in our sanctification. He calls us to look less and less like the world.

The last plea I will make, especially for you new Christians, is please, don't get scared because the joy in the freedom of Christianity is in this process, one step at a time. As you open doors and as you get rid of the patchwork quilt and as you relinquish yourselves to God and to his enabling, to his strength, and his leading, you can take one step at a time. As Paul tells the Corinthians, you will be changed from one degree of glory to the next.

I talked with someone earlier who became a Christian last week. I asked if this was too much. She said, "No, I know what lies ahead; I'm excited!" I hope that is your response as well. We are going to fail; it's not a good thing, but God is there. If we are confessing our sin, he is forgiving our sin. He gives us the Holy Spirit to help us to obey him. Then he calls us to present our bodies sacrificially to him so that we are not conformed to this world but transformed by the renewing of our minds; this is God's will for our lives and our sanctification.

So the questions simply are, "Is your life changing? Is your life beginning to change? Is your life continuing to change? Are you, one step at a time, becoming a fully devoted disciple of Jesus Christ?" I pray that you are.

11

Walking Together

OUR NEW FAMILY

When you and I became Christians, we walked through the gates of heaven, as it were, one person at a time; no family plan. We don't get into heaven because of mom and dad or uncles or aunts; we walk through one person at a time. Yet on the other side of that gate lies our new family; a family with whom we can walk together as we go through life and a family where we have a new father and new brothers.

It's interesting that the word "brothers" is the most common way in which the New Testament refers to believers, men and women alike. We are brothers; we are a family that is not broken down based on gender or race or class. We are a family that is bound together by love for our Father, and then that love for our Father flows through him out to one another. It is in fact this loving unity that is to characterize the family of God, which proclaims Jesus to the world.

In John 17, Jesus is praying to God for the church, and in verse 21, his prayer is: "that they," meaning you and me, "may all be one, just as you, Father, are in me, and I in you, that they also may be in us," Why then is that so important? "So that the world may believe that you have sent me. The glory that you have given me I have given to them, that they may be one even as We are one." Then Jesus repeats himself in verse 23: "I in them and you in me, that they may become perfectly one, so that the world may know that you sent me and loved them even as you loved me."

That is what biblical community is all about; as you and I are bound together in our love, people will look at us and they will say, "Oh how they love God." When people look at us, they will see the Father's love in us and see that in truth. God did send his Son to the world. All of this is tied up in the fact that you and I are the family of God. We are to be an authentic, biblical community.

CHALLENGE OF AUTHENTIC, BIBLICAL COMMUNITY

Because this authentic biblical community is so important, it should come as no surprise to any of us that there are great challenges in creating it. If it's really this important and if it is God's way of showing his love and drawing people to himself, certainly we're going to expect great challenges in community.

The American Culture (and this is an American phenomenon — perhaps partly European — but it is primarily our phenomenon) is one of individualism and of isolationism; it is not one of community. Gallup, in his polls, has shown time and time again that Americans are among the loneliest people on the earth; we have more toys than anybody, but no one with whom to play — this culture of fragmentation and isolation is lonely.

Circles of relationships

In *The Connecting Church*, a book I recommend that you read, the author, Randy Frazee, talks a lot about the fact that we have many disconnected circles of relationships. The circle of relationships that we call the church. The circle of relationships that we call work. The circle of relationships that we call family.

We also have the circles of relationships connected with our kids: soccer teams, basketball teams, neighborhood stuff, Girl Scouts. The list goes on and on; we have many circles of relationships and so many of them are not connected. So the very thing that we crave the most, authentic deep relationships built upon the redeeming work of Jesus Christ, we will never find because we are so busy living fragmented, disconnected lives without margin. The American culture is one of isolation; it is not one of community.

Changing culture

In his book, Frazee goes on to document the cultural changes in America over the last 100 years. What I enjoyed in reading this book were all the things that I take for granted, but then I realized that there was a shift, a change, from when I was a kid. He talks, as many sociologists do, about the flight of rural America into the depersonalized, big, urban centers in this country. He talks about how we used to sit on the porch and talk to people when they came by; but now instead, we sit inside our air-conditioned homes or perhaps go outside on our private back decks. We also used to walk to neighborhood stores, but now we drive to superstores. In fact, now we can go through the speed checkout and not even talk to a cashier. We used to walk around the block and now we have treadmills in our basements and our bedrooms so we can watch the news. We used to go to the post office; as fast as it is, there's usually a line. Now there are televisions that we can look at so that we don't have to talk to anyone as we stand in line. We are getting to the point where we never really have to leave the house; we can shop on the Internet and not even pay sales tax.

In his book, Frazee talks about a man named Robert Putnam, a Harvard professor who did some research, and his research shows that Americans entertain friends at home 45% less often in the late 90s than they did in the mid to late 70s. He also uncovered the rather shocking fact that between 1974 and 1998, the frequency with which Americans spent "a social evening with someone who lives in your neighborhood" fell by about one third. The home has become a place of solitary confinement. However, even this characteristic is nearly lost as the home has become, for many, simply a boarding house where people occasionally eat and mostly just sleep. The other day, there was a plea to American families to function "as families." The plea was that if we could just do this, it would be one of the greatest thing we could do — have at least one meal a week together.

We live in an individualistic, fragmented, lonely culture, and yet the problem is that we were built for community. When God made Adam, he looked at him and said, "It's not good that he's alone." We weren't made for isolation. What is true of the intimate relationships is also true with larger social units, the social units of family and the family of God, so God created the church to meet that deep need of community, which is inside of every one of us.

MODEL OF THE EARLY CHURCH — ALL ABOUT GOD

Certainly, as we look at the model of the early church in Acts 2, we can see exactly what God intended for us to be like. Here is the description of the early church in Acts 2:42. "And they devoted themselves to the apostles' teaching and fellowship, to the breaking of bread and the prayers. And awe came upon every soul, and many wonders and signs were being done through the apostles. And all who believed were together and had all things in common. And they were selling their possessions and belongings and distributing the proceeds to all, as any had need. And day by day, attending the temple together and breaking bread in their homes, they received their food with glad and generous hearts, praising God and having favor with all the people. And the Lord added to their number day by day those who were being saved."

Center of our lives

When we look at this picture of the early church, we start to get a taste for what God wants community to look like; it starts first and foremost with God. God is in the absolute center; it's all about God. God pervades everything that they did: they devoted themselves to the prayers; they were praising God; they were involved in evangelism and people were being saved; day by day, they were involved in worship where they were attending the temple together. Jesus and God were the absolute center, the absolute focus, of the early church and he pervaded everything that they did.

If God is not the center of this family, then we are nothing more than friends and casual acquaintances; that is all we are. Without God, there cannot be anything else; we're just a social club and a community center. However, it's because God is our Father that therefore you and I can truly be brothers, not divided by gender or by race or by class; it's all about God, and he is in the absolute center.

As we read the story of the early church, we quickly realize that if God truly is the center, both independently and corporately, then this very fact is going to have to push itself out, flowing in different directions. You can't just love God and do nothing else. I love the fact that when they asked Jesus, "What's the greatest commandment?" He answers, "You shall love the Lord your God with all your heart and with all your soul and with all your strength and with all your mind, and the second is just like it, you shall love your neighbor as yourself'" (Luke 10:27). I don't like that translation; it actually means that you shall love the "other person" as yourself. We can't love God and he can't be the center of our lives without it's flowing out into other areas of our lives — it's absolutely impossible, and Jesus makes that clear. There are at least three different directions out of which our relationship with God and our love for him flows.

1. Growth into spiritual maturity

One way in which our love for God flows is into the area of spiritual maturity, both individually and corporately. As you and I love God, we will learn more about what he is like. In order to be like Jesus, we must find out what Jesus is like, and then we will learn and grow. This is why the early church devoted themselves to the apostles' teaching; this is the whole area of discipleship and growth.

In Colossians 1, Paul is reviewing his ministry to the Colossian Church. He talks about how his goal for their lives was that they grow up — that they mature. In Colossians 1:28, Paul says, "him," meaning Christ, "we proclaim, warning everyone and teaching everyone with all wisdom in order that we may present everyone mature in Christ." That is his goal, maturity in Christ. Then Paul adds, "For this I toil" (now watch the pronouns), "struggling with all his energy that he powerfully works within me." This is one of the ways in which the centrality of Christ in our lives and in this church pushes itself out.

We must grow in our knowledge and then be transformed by that knowledge; therefore, we are committed to biblical preaching; there will never be any other kind of preaching from this pulpit, and that is our commitment. Growth into spiritual maturity is why this year in the adult Sunday school classes, we're going to go through a systematic theology so that we can learn and be challenged. This is why we have the Biblical Training Institute on Wednesday nights so that you can learn enough to call yourselves biblically literate. This is why, among many missions efforts, we support BiblicalTraining.org, an online school giving away a seminary education to the world. These are all different ways in which we are taking seriously the fact that, as God is the center of our lives, one of the ways in which that is going to affect us is our desire to grow into maturity — to train and be trained.

2. Devoted to fellowship

The centrality of Christ also pushes its way out in a second way, and that is in the whole area of fellowship. The Acts 2 Church devoted themselves to fellowship; they didn't kind of pick and choose, did they? They devoted themselves to fellowship; day by day, they were breaking bread in their homes. I think as we read this passage, it's fair to say that the church was the social center of their lives. The circle of relationships in that church was the central set of relationships in their lives.

"Christian crockpot"

I've often encouraged you with the idea of the "Christian Crockpot." The idea is to get up Sunday morning and throw a bigger roast in the crockpot, a couple more potatoes, a couple more carrots, and a couple cans of soup. (The crockpot got me through seminary!) It's not hard to do, just turn it on medium when you leave. You go to church and you look for someone you don't recognize and you say, "This isn't natural; you're my brother. Come on over, and let's get to know each other." What do you call a family where siblings don't know each other? I call it dysfunctional.

So also in the family of God, we must be devoted to fellowship and that's why God made crockpots! (Not really!) May I encourage you to buy an oversized crockpot and then use it? When I was in graduate school in Scotland, one of the most influential families was a family who, every Sunday, would look for someone they did not know in the church and invite them over. (They always picked the students up, too, and brought us over because they felt so sorry for us! We had very sad faces.) Her ministry was to entertain, to make people feel welcome, and to say, "Welcome into my family." We had this Sunday meal together so much of the time.

Primary social circle

May I encourage you to make the family of God the primary social circle in your lives? Again, may I encourage you to make the family of God your primary social set of relationships, because as long as we have many, many circles of relationships that are disconnected and our lives are fragmented, we will never deal with the loneliness that is in our lives. We will never have a sense of connection because we're scattered all over the place.

One of the things that Frazee is really encouraging us to do is to narrow our scope of circles. We can have friends outside the church (hopefully we all have non-Christian friends outside the church), but may church be the primary social circle of our lives.

I would love to see the day in which this church building is full every single hour. I would love to see when you young moms are going a little crazy with the kids, to call up another young mom that's going crazy and say, "Let's meet at church for coffee." We always have coffee here at church! While you're here, let your kids run rampant; you can clean up when you're done. Have coffee together, talk together, share your lives together, and be encouraged by one another.

I look forward to the day when my son comes home and says, "Dad, let's play basketball (which he loves to do because he can always beat me now). So instead of going to a gym, we would say, "let's go to church to play; in fact, let's call someone up and let's have him and his son come, too. We'll set up the hoop in the gym and we'll play together."

I would love to see the day when those of you who have moved into retirement from teaching all of your lives, which means you now really have time to serve the family of God, say, "I've taught math and science for 40 years, I'll be in the

Library from 2-4. If your kids are struggling, bring them by; I would love to share my life's experience with them, my young brothers." Retirement means now you really have time to serve the family of God.

I can see that day when these things happen, but it's not going to happen until we become devoted to fellowship, and that means making this church body the center of our relational lives.

Grace

Authentic biblical community is a lot more than just the fun times and the sharing times; as important as those times are. If we are going to be devoted to fellowship, I think it means that this place will have to become a haven of grace. I've been reading Philip Yancey's amazing book, *What's so Amazing About Grace?* I would encourage you to read this book. Through the pages, Yancey is trying to define what it means for God to treat us with grace. He says that God's grace means that there's nothing that I can do to make God love me more, and grace means there's nothing I can do to make God love me less. God doesn't love me for who I am; God simply loves me. He is a God of grace to me. Oh that you and I should become receivers and givers of that kind of grace!

This is where all the "one anothers" come in Scripture. Scripture says: We are to live in harmony with one another. We are to not pass judgment on one another. We are to not speak evil of one another. We are to encourage one another. We are to show hospitality to one another. We are to bear one another's burdens. As Paul says in Ephesians 4:32: "Be kind, tenderhearted, forgiving one another as God in Christ has forgiven you." It's impossible to be obedient to God in isolation. It is absolutely impossible to be an obedient Christian and live in isolation. If we're off living by ourselves, how can we bear one another's burdens? If we refuse to gather together, how can we show compassion to one another? It's impossible.

What it means to be devoted to fellowship is to have God central in our lives, not us, not our jobs, not our wealth (which is really God's), not our fame, not our fortune, but God. If God is truly central in this life of ours, we will push out and we will be devoted to fellowship, just like the early church was devoted to fellowship.

3. Ministry

In Acts, there is a third way in which we see that the centrality of Christ pushes its way out into their lives, and that is in the whole area of ministry. If God is central in our lives and if God is central in the family of God, then it will show itself in service and outreach.

Within the body

The centrality of God will show itself, first of all, in service to the body. In Hebrews 10:24, the author says, "Let us consider how to stir up one another to love and good works." That's a great way to say it. Let's sit down and think through how we can go about encouraging and stirring up one another, to love one another, and to do good things. Let's be deliberate about this, and think it through. "Not neglecting to meet together, as is the habit of some, but encouraging one another." This is why Paul repeatedly says that all the gifts that are given to the church: the gifts of ministry, the gifts of service, the gifts of preaching and teaching and showing mercy and giving and having faith.

All of these gifts were given for the edification of the body for the common good; they were given to you and me so that together we can serve one another; we can serve the body of Christ. That includes our finances, which was certainly one of the outstanding features of the early church. God was so central in who they were that while they weren't commanded to sell everything, they did, and they shared with the people. I know people often think, "It doesn't say that I have to sell everything"; that is true, yet there are many other passages that perhaps give us cause to think.

For example, in 1 John 3:16, John writes, "By this we know love, that he," meaning Jesus, "laid down his life for us, and we ought to lay down our lives for the brothers." What does it look like in practical application? "If anyone has the world's goods and sees his brother in need, yet closes his heart against him, how does God's love abide in him?" The answer is, "It can't!" If you and I love God, we, of necessity, must love the other person. "Little children, let us not love in word or talk but in deed and in truth." In other words, talk is cheap.

Outside the body

If God is central in our lives individually and corporately, it will push itself out into ministry, into service for the body, and also into service outside the body; this is what missions and evangelism is all about. As you and I are pervaded and unified by the love of God, as our love for him grows and spreads out so that you love me and I love you, people will look at us and say, "Boy, they're different; look at how they love Jesus; that message of the cross must be true."

This is the goal that Jesus sets up in John 17; it is something that comes out of community. As you and I live in community, we show Christ to be sweet to the world. People will respond to us in the same way they responded in Acts 2 — we will have favor with all people. People will be saved and will be added to us.

HARD WORK

Community is hard work. If you're reflecting on what I'm saying, this is not some light, easy task that comes naturally; it's radical and counter-cultural — just like Jesus and just like the early church. Paul says, "For this I toil." Toil is a word that refers specifically to manual labor that is used as if we were going to go out and dig a ditch. "For this I toil and yet I am struggling, not by my energy but by his energy that he is working powerfully within me and through me" (Colossians 1:29). Community stuff is hard work.

Begins with a common purpose

Community begins with a common purpose; that's where it all starts. This church is neither a community center nor a social club. It is not a place where you can come and have your spiritual sensitivities tickled. This is the family of God that is here for one central purpose, and that is to glorify God in everything that we say and do and don't say and don't do.

I love the illustration of A. W. Tozer when he says, "How do you tune one hundred pianos so that they can all play together? You don't tune them to each other; you tune them to the same tuning fork." As our lives are focused on one tuning fork, and that is God, it pervades our lives so that we say and do only what will advance the kingdom of God, even in our eating and drinking, Paul tells the Corinthians. Do whatever you do with your driving purpose to glorify God; that's our common purpose; that's the tie that binds us together; not the fact that we meet in the same building. It's God who is central. If our commitment to God is central in our lives, it must fan out into at least these three different areas of discipleship, fellowship and ministry.

SIMPLIFY YOUR LIFE

May I encourage you to simplify all your life, even as I struggle to simplify my life? I've been faced with this issue that I have to simplify my life. Again, I encourage all of you to read Randy Frazee's book, *The Connecting Church*, because it's a very convicting book along those lines.

May I also encourage all of us to make these, our brothers, the central set of relationships in our lives? Has anyone here lived in a natural family where there has never been conflict? I'm not seeing any hands. When conflict comes, what do we do? Do we run away and hide? I encourage all of us to work through it, to lean into it, to grow from it, and not to turn tail and run. We need to be kind to one another, tenderhearted to one another, forgiving one another; just as God in Christ forgave you, so also you and I should forgive others.

BECOME A "HAVEN OF GRACE"

If we do that, then in God's way and in God's timing, we will become that haven of grace, that place of honest, open, authentic relationships where the masks come down, where we have freely received grace from God, where we have freely received grace from one another, so in turn we extend it back, where we bear one another's burdens, where we encourage one another towards holiness, a place where loneliness will no longer be, but instead a place where that deep sense of belonging that is built into all of us will be satisfied.

More importantly, though, we will be a place where people

come in and they look at us and say, "How they love Jesus! Jesus must be who he said he is. He must be the answer to the problems in my life. He must be the solution to my sin." This is a radical and counter-cultural way of looking at life. It's especially radical for Americans to look at Acts 2 and say, "Let's be that kind of church," radical and counter-cultural, just like Jesus was radical and counter-cultural.

12

Inviting Others to Walk with You

Jesus calls people to "Follow me." He calls people to "Walk with me." You and I are followers; we are disciples of Jesus Christ. To the first disciples, he said, "Follow me and I will make you fish for people." Part of fishing for people is to invite them to fish for more people; all disciples are to fish; all disciples are to encourage others to walk with them.

MAKE MORE DISCIPLES

In the final words of the Gospel of Matthew, Jesus gives what is called his "Great Commission," a commission that is true for all disciples. In Matthew 28:18, he says, "All authority in heaven and on earth has been given to me. Go therefore and make disciples of all nations, baptizing them in the name of the Father and of the Son and of the Holy Spirit, teaching them to observe all that I have commanded you. And behold, I am with you always, to the end of the age."

The command, the invitation, for all disciples is that we make more disciples; we are to be involved in evangelizing and baptizing them. We also are to be involved in people becoming fully devoted disciples of Jesus Christ by teaching them to observe absolutely everything that Jesus has taught.

Paul uses different metaphors, he talks about the fact that we are ambassadors for Christ. In 2 Corinthians 5:19, he tells the church in Corinth, "in Christ, God was reconciling the world to himself, not counting their trespasses against them, but entrusting to us the message of reconciliation." God has entrusted to us the amazing Gospel, that there is the way to be friends with God. "Therefore, we are ambassadors for Christ, God making his appeal through us." So Paul makes that appeal. "We implore you on behalf of Christ, be reconciled to God. For our sake God made him Christ to be sin who knew no sin, so that in him," in Jesus, "we might become the righteousness of God." All disciples are invited to invite others to walk with them, to walk with Jesus. All disciples are to be self-replicating — or to say it differently, Christians are in the business of cloning.

REGENERATION

This should be the most natural thing in our lives. What I want to do is walk through this process with you, to show that this isn't frightening. We don't have to have an M.Div. or some other degree. This is simply for disciples and it's an absolutely natural process because that process began at conversion. In conversion, God changed us, that's the doctrine of regeneration, and changed people live changed lives. We've talked about the fact that things can't continue as they were before; you and I have been given a new birth; you and I have been given a new life; we have been made into new creatures; we are part of a new creation. Our lives must be different; changed people simply live in a changed way. As you and I start to live out our changed lives, people are going to start to notice.

People will notice

In Philippians 2:14, Paul says, "Do all things without grumbling or questioning, in order that you may be blameless and innocent, children of God without blemish in the midst of a crooked and twisted generation, among whom you shine as lights in the world, holding fast to the word of life." We do truly live in a crooked, twisted, and perverse generation. Yet as you and I live out our lives, we are going to live it out as lights of the world, holding fast to the word of life, and people are going to start to notice that there's something different about us.

Jesus uses other metaphors to make the point — you and I are the lights of the world. In Matthew 5:14, Jesus says, "You are the light of the world." Then he builds a couple of images to help us understand. "A city set on a hill cannot be hidden."

You can take a city, and when you turn its lights on and stick it up on top of a hill, you're going to see it. "Nor do people light a lamp and put it under a basket, but on a stand, and it gives light to all in the house." What's the point of lighting a light and then hiding it? We're not going to light a light and then stick it under something; the whole point of lighting a light is so that it will illuminate the room.

Then in verse 16, Jesus drives the point home: "In the same way, let your light shine before others, so that they may see your good words and give glory to your Father who is in heaven." You and I are the city on the hill; we are the light that has been lit in order to illuminate the room; as we live out this kind of life, we're different, and people will see it and notice that there's something different. In the preceding verse, Matthew 5:13, Jesus uses a different metaphor, which is that of salt. He says, "You are the salt of the earth, but if salt has lost its taste, how shall its saltiness be restored? It is no longer good for anything except to be thrown out and trampled under people's feet." We know that salt technically cannot lose its taste, but what Jesus is actually talking about is salt being defiled; we can dilute salt with other substances so it loses its ability to preserve.

The point Jesus is making is that Christians don't live in isolation from the world. He has just finished the beatitudes, and they're so strong that there might be this temptation to think, "I need to live separate from the world." Jesus says, "No, Christians don't live in isolation from the world." Just as salt was used to preserve meat, so also Jesus (quoting one commentator) "calls his disciples to arrest corruption and prevent moral decay in their world"; that's the function of us being the salt of the earth. Just as salt can become mixed with various impure substances, thereby becoming worthless as a preservative, so also Christians can mix themselves with the things of the world and become worthless as agents of change and redemption. You and I are the salt of the earth; we are agents of change and redemption, and we are here to arrest corruption and to prevent moral decay, just as salt keeps meat from going bad.

As you and I live as salt to the earth and lights of the world, people will notice that we're different; this is the kind of changed lives that changed people live.

I like the King James translation of Titus 2:14; it uses an English word in a way we don't any longer. Jesus says that he "gave himself for us that he might redeem us from all iniquity and purify unto himself a *peculiar* people, zealous of good works." Now, 400 or 500 years ago in English, the word peculiar meant special. What Jesus was doing was purifying for himself a people who were special to him — those who are his people. However, I often think of us as a rather odd lot of people. You and I, to the eyes of world, are just a little peculiar and that's okay. In fact, that is the way it must be. We're living changed lives and people are supposed to notice that our lives are different.

People will wonder

As people start to notice that you and I are a tad peculiar, they're going to start asking the question, "What is it that makes these people different?" There's a quotation that some people say Martin Luther said and some people say St. Francis of Assisi said; I don't know, but it's a great quote: "Preach at all times. If necessary, use words." Our lives preach louder and our deeds proclaim truer than any words could ever say. People will see our changed lives and they will start to wonder, "What's different about them?"

One of the more powerful examples of this in Scripture is Peter's instruction to wives, specifically to wives who are married to non-Christians. In 1 Peter 3:1 he says, "Likewise, wives, be submissive to your own husbands, so that even if some do not obey the word," if they don't respond to the spoken Gospel message, "they may be won without a word by the conduct of their wives when they see your respectful and pure conduct. Do not let your adorning be external — the braiding of hair, the wearing of gold, the putting on of clothing, but let your adorning be the hidden person of the heart with the imperishable beauty of a gentle and quiet spirit." Peter tells these wives that the way to win husbands to the Lord is not to preach at them or not put all emphasis on the externals of beauty, but rather to focus on the internal beauty of women of God. Wives are to be those who are gentle — the very way in which they live their lives will speak volumes.

People will respond

As people start to notice how you and I live out our changed
Christian lives, they will start to wonder, "What's so different about them?" Eventually, what's going to happen is that
they will respond to the witness of our lives one of two ways.
This is a great verse, 2 Corinthians 2:14, where Paul uses the
powerful image of smell to make his point that there are two
ways that people are going to respond to the witness of your
life. Paul writes, "But thanks be to God, who in Christ always
leads us in triumphal procession, and through us spreads
the fragrance of the knowledge of him everywhere." There
is your changed life. "For we are the aroma of Christ to God
among those who are being saved and among those who are
perishing." In other words, we smell differently to different
people; to one, a fragrance from death to death; to the other, a
fragrance from life to life.

As you and I live out our changed lives, to some people
we are going to be the aroma of life. This is again what Jesus
was talking about back in Matthew 5:16. "Let your light shine
before others, so that they may see your good works and give
glory to your Father who is in heaven." To some, we will be
the aroma of life; but to others, we will be the stench of death,
their death. In 1 Peter 4:3-5, he writes, "For the time that is
past," the time prior to your conversion, "suffices for doing
what the Gentiles want to do, living in sensuality, passions,
drunkenness, orgies, drinking parties, and lawless idolatry.
With respect to this, they," your past non-Christian friends,
"are surprised when you do not join them in the same flood
of debauchery and they malign you; but they will give account to him who is ready to judge the living and the dead."

To some, we will be the aroma of life; and to others, we
will be the stench of death. Our non-Christian friends will
see our changed lives and they will not understand and they
will malign us.

People will ask why

The key in this whole living-out-our-lives-as-followers-of-Je-
sus natural process is that if we smell like the aroma of life,
then they will ask us why. People will come to us and they
will say, "Why do you smell so good?" They probably won't

use that metaphor, but that's what they're asking. "Why do you smell so good?" Paul tells the Colossian Church in 4:5-6, "Conduct yourselves wisely toward outsiders, making the best use of the time. Let your speech always be gracious, seasoned with salt, so that you may know how you ought to answer each person." Paul is saying that as we live out our different lives, our speech will be gracious, not cutting, condemning, judgmental, or critical. Our speech is going to be gracious, and they're going to want to know, "Why are you so gracious?" We need to know how to answer each of these people, and the question simply is: "Are you and I ready to tell them why we smell so good?"

HOW DO I RESPOND?

Share personal testimony

In 1 Peter 3:15-16, he says, "always being prepared to make a defense to anyone who asks you for a reason for the hope that is in you." People look at us and they should see that we have a hope that they don't have. "Yet do it with gentleness and respect, having a good conscience." What we're talking about here is the whole issue of, what in the church has historically been called, "having a personal testimony"; being able to share our stories. I'm not talking about how we would share our faith with someone who doesn't know us, who we might run into on a bus or something, although that's important. What I'm talking about is our having a testimony that we can share with the people whom we know. When they see that our lives are different, that we have a gracious speech, and that we have a hope that they don't have, how are we going be able to tell them why we have this hope and why our speech is so gracious. This is the issue of friendship evangelism.

There are some powerful images and stories in the Bible about personal testimonies. I think one of the most powerful is the story in John 9, where Jesus heals the man who had been born blind (the whole chapter is about this story). The religious leaders are all bent out of shape, and they're not willing to say that Jesus was the one who gave him sight, so they go through this foolish repetitive set of questions. They get his parents in and ask them.

Then finally, in verse 24, "So for the second time they called the man who had been blind and said to him, 'Give glory to God. We know that this man is a sinner.'" What they mean is that Jesus doesn't follow all of their religious rituals, so he is a sinner; he cannot have possibly healed him. So then in verse 25, the blind man answered, "Whether he is a sinner I do not know. One thing I do know, that though I was blind, now I see."

Powerful personal testimony is really hard to argue against, such as "Once I was blind." or "Once I was dead in my sin, unable to see God or what was right; unable to see what righteousness was." or "I was dead and had no hope, but now I can see." We would just simply have to write the person off as a complete cuckoo case. The religious leaders kicked the blind man out of the Temple and had nothing to do with him; they thought there was something seriously wrong with him.

Another good testimony is in Acts 4, where the young church had been witnessing to the risen Jesus and the religious leaders were unhappy (what a shock). In chapter 4, they bring Peter and James in to defend themselves. Starting at verse 19, "But Peter and John answered them, 'Whether it is right in the sight of God to listen to you rather than to God, you must judge,' in other words, I really don't care what you think, 'for we cannot but speak of what we have seen and heard.'" This shows the power of personal testimony. You and I both need to be prepared to have a personal testimony.

Let me just give some practical tips along this line. The first practical tip is the well-known acronym of KISS: Keep It Simple Stupid. Personal testimonies don't have to be complicated; they don't have to be this long, drawn-out, well-crafted, logical treatise because that's not what saved us and it's not what's going to save anyone else — keep it simple.

Share with them what your life was like before you became a follower of Jesus; if you do this, my encouragement is to keep it minimal. I've heard some personal testimonies that were 90% of what a rotten jerk they were before conversion; it's like they are glorying in past sin. Tell people what your life was like before Christ, but don't glory in it; keep it to a minimum. Tell them why you decided to become disciples of Jesus Christ. Perhaps you may even want to relay the details of your conversion experience. Then share with them the difference it has made in your life. "I once was blind but now I see!" Keep it simple.

Our personal testimonies are something that we can prepare and practice beforehand; I would encourage all of you to practice them. Find ways to communicate the truths of our lives to people within 3 to 5 minutes, but again keep it simple.

Invite them to walk with you

Please understand that our personal testimonies are only the first step. If somebody comes up to us and says, "You smell so good. You have the smell of life about you. Your speech is seasoned; it is gracious, "if we were to simply tell them why our lives have changed and then stop, we haven't finished. We must go to the next step of inviting them to walk with us because you and I are all fishermen. You must be prepared and I must be prepared; having told our testimonies, and perhaps woven into our testimonies the very plan of salvation, we can then share with them how they too can be followers of Jesus Christ.

ABC

There are many methods out there for sharing salvation. I tend to use the ABCs; I'm sure you've noticed. What does it mean to be a Christian? Being a Christian means to:

A. Admit that you're a sinner and you're separated from God; acknowledge that his evaluation of you is right.

B. Believe in your heart that Jesus is God, he is Savior, and he is Lord — he is who he says he is. Believe that he did what he said he was going to do — die on the cross for the forgiveness of our sin.

Then, C. Commit your life to him. He's not only our Savior, but he is also our Lord. There, I did it in about 50 seconds!

John 3:16

Perhaps we want to get used to using John 3:16 as I did in the first talk of this series. Find a way to say, "God loved the world. He created the world but it was separated from him by sin and yet he still loved it. He loved it so much that he gave his only Son. Jesus is the only sacrifice for sin. Jesus is the only way that this alienated world can ever be reconciled to its Creator again. Whoever believes in him — it's not simply enough to have intellectual assent, but you must commit your life and belief to him. Then you will not perish, but you will live forever. You will live a new kind of life, an eternal kind of life, that doesn't start when you die, but it starts right now. John says that we have already passed from death into life. Perhaps we might want to use John 3:16 as a way to share.

Romans

Perhaps we would want to use those three famous verses in Romans. Actually, some people like to carry a small Bible with them and have these three verses underlined; they've memorized them so they can turn to them and actually have the other person read the verses.

Read Romans 3:23. "For all have sinned and fall short of the glory of God." Every one of us has missed the mark. Every one of us has failed to do what our Creator has called us to do."

Turn to Romans 6:23. "For the wages of sin is death," which is the penalty for living separated from a holy God, "but the free gift of God is eternal life through Jesus Christ our Lord." The only way to get to heaven and the only way to have our sin forgiven is through the work of Jesus Christ and it's a free gift. There's nothing that you can do; no religion or no amount of good activity can earn your way to heaven; it is the free gift of God.

Romans 10:9. "If you confess with your mouth that Jesus is Lord, if you believe in your heart that God raised him from the dead, then you shall be saved." Your assurance is that God has committed that if we confess Jesus is who he says he is and he has done what he has said he would do, then you shall be saved. These three are probably the most famous verses in the entire book of Romans, which contains the whole plan of salvation, with which we can share with someone in two minutes.

Metaphors

It's always helpful for non-propositional people to have illustrations. I'm a propositional person, so I don't think in terms of metaphors. Some of you are helping me to learn to think metaphorically. The most common illustration for salvation is that there is this great chasm, the Grand Canyon, and we and our sin are over here, and God and his forgiveness is over there. The chasm is so great that there's nothing we can do to get over to where God is. So the cross comes down and it fills the chasm through the work of the only Son of God, who then invites us across to live in the full presence of God the Father forever.

Illustrations are good and they're powerful, and we can mix and match these things. We must be prepared as we share our personal testimonies to move beyond our testimonies and to become fishers of men, saying, "you too can have this hope that I have; here's how you can do it."It's as simple as ABC.

PRACTICAL ADVICE

Focus on Jesus

I have some practical advice. Be sure to keep your focus on Jesus because it's so easy to become distracted. The issue isn't our being religious; the issue isn't our good deeds; the issue isn't our being able to answer their intellectual questions. (Very few people actually have intellectual questions. Most people's problem with God is moral, not intellectual.) Your story isn't really the issue either; the issue is Jesus. We must stay focused on who Jesus is — he is God; he is Savior; he is Lord. We must stay focused on what Jesus has done — he has died on the cross to pay the penalty for our sin. As we develop our personal testimonies and learn to share the Gospel, make sure the focus isn't on us; but make sure the focus stays where it belongs — on Jesus.

Don't accept too much responsibility

As we try to put this whole issue of personal testimony into action, please don't accept too much responsibility. One of the reasons I think people get frightened is that we tend to assume too much responsibility in this whole process. Do we know why some people think we smell so good? Do we know why we are the aroma of life to some of our friends who are watching our actions? Look at our friends and think, "These people don't like me; these people are drawn to me. What's the difference? Why are these people drawn to me?" Are they drawn to us because we have powerful stories or compelling arguments? No, that's not what's going on at all.

Jesus says in John 6:44 that "no one can come to the Father unless he draws them." The point is that God is at work in the lives of these people, and he is drawing people to himself. So when someone looks at us and says, "you smell good," it's not because of us, it's because God is at work in their lives — he's drawing people to himself.

There is balance in all of this. I'm not saying that we should totally be passive. I don't think that there's normally a time where we've shared our stories and then we should just leave it and wonder if they're going to ask us how to be saved. There certainly is a time when we have to take the initiative. We can say, "Would you like to have the same hope that I have? Would you like to have the same power at work in you that is at work in me?" You don't want to push this; there is a balance to all this, but certainly there's a time in which we can ask them the question. There also will be times in which it is obvious that they want to know themselves.

Don't become the Holy Spirit

Don't become the Holy Spirit; it's his job to convict people of their sin (John 16:8), not ours. As we are sharing our lives with people, if they're turned off, there is nothing we can do about it because they're dead in their trespasses and sin and only God can quicken, or enliven, their spirits. Do not accept responsibility that is only God's. Paul Little writes, "It is the Holy Spirit, not we, who converts an individual. We, the privileged ambassadors of Jesus Christ, can communicate a verbal message. We can demonstrate through our personality and life what the grace of Jesus Christ can accomplish, but let us never naively think that we have converted a soul and brought him to Jesus Christ. No one calls Jesus 'Lord' except by the Holy Spirit." If you and I share, then we have never failed; we only fail when we don't share. When we share, we've done our part. It's not our job to convict people of their sin; it's not our job to save them; it is not our job to convert them.

If they reject us, what does Jesus say? They are not rejecting us, they are rejecting Jesus. If they reject Jesus, then they are rejecting the one who sent Jesus. So when they are rejecting us, they are not rejecting us; in fact, Jesus says very clearly that when they reject us, we are blessed. Right after the Beatitudes, Matthew 5:11-12 says, "Blessed are you when others revile you and persecute you and utter all kinds of evil against you falsely on My account. Rejoice and be glad, for your reward is great in heaven, for so they persecuted the prophets who were before you." You never fail and I never fail if we share; the rest is up to God. The fact of the matter is Christians are the great cloners of all time, bar none. We were changed in conversion and changed people live changed lives. To some we stink; that's fine, but to some we smell wonderful and we are to be prepared to tell them why. As soon as we tell them why, we must ask the most fundamental question, "Would you like to join this journey of real life with me? Would you like to be a follower of Jesus Christ, a child of God? Let me tell you how." Then let God be God and do what only God can do, and that is give life to the dead — this is most natural thing in the world for a Christian.

BiblicalTraining.org

BiblicalTraining.org is not-for-profit ministry that gives all people access to a world-class Christian education. Our classes range from new believers to biblical literacy ("Foundations"), leadership development ("Leadership"), and seminary-level training ("Institute"). These three programs of study insure that your education is systematic and complete. We encourage holistic transformation through mentor/apprentice relationships, learning in community, using the head/heart/hands model. All Bible classes are taught by world-class professors from major seminaries, and we now offer over 1,000 hours in over 90 classes. Our curriculum can even be customized to meet the specific needs of your church or ministry.

DISTINCTIVES

1. **World class**. Our professors are among the best academics in the world, and know how to teach.
2. **Holistic**. We want to see students move through content to deep reflection and application.
3. **Configurable**. Ministries can use BT lectures as well as their own to design their educational program.
4. **Accessible**. BiblicalTraining is a web-based ministry whose content is free.
5. **Community-based**. We encourage people to learn together, in mentor/apprentice relationships.
6. **Broadly evangelical**. Our materials are broadly evangelical, governed by our Statement of Faith.
7. **Partners**. We provide the content and delivery mechanisms, and our partners provide the community and mentoring. When there are no partners, we hope to provide a virtual community and real-life mentors.

Made in the USA
Coppell, TX
17 January 2023

11282414R00085